OFFICIAL OPRY® PICTURE-HISTORY BOOK

TABLE OF CONTENTS

D0992747

Jerry Strobel, Editor
Photographer: Donnie Beauchamp

Copyright: 1994 Gaylord Entertainment Company
Nashville, Tennessee
Volume 9 Edition 2
Price $6.00

Bill, Bill Monroe and Opry President Hal Durham share a humorous moment during ceremonies dedicating the Grand Ole Opry Museum.

When Bill Anderson visited Nashville in May 1958 as WSM Radio's Mr. DJ, USA, he was on the other side of the microphone interviewing Grand Ole Opry members. In July 1961 he stepped onto the Opry stage as a member of the world famous radio show.

"Whisperin' Bill" Anderson wears many hats. The singer, songwriter, record producer, businessman, soap-opera actor, game-show host and avid sports fan was watching the All-Star baseball game on TV when the call came inviting him to join the Opry, he recalls.

A Columbia, S.C., native, Bill grew up in Georgia and holds a degree in journalism from the University of Georgia. A former newspaperman, he broke into the music business as a disc jockey at a small radio station in Georgia and since has become one of show business' most honored men.

During the course of his Country Music career, Bill has had 72 single records of his own on the charts and countless hundreds of songs he wrote that were recorded by other artists. He has released nearly 50 albums, won more than 50 BMI songwriting awards (more than any other writer in the history of Country Music), been named Male Vocalist of the Year, was half of the Duet of the Year with two different singing partners (Jan Howard and Mary Lou Turner), was named Songwriter of the Year several times, wrote the Song of the Year and twice recorded the Record of the Year.

Counted among his hits are "Tips of My Fingers," "Po' Folks," "Still," "City Lights," "I May Never Get To Heaven," "When Two Worlds Collide," "I Can't Wait Any Longer," "Where Have All the Heroes Gone" and "Still The One." His latest albums for Curb Records are: "Best of Bill Anderson" and "Country Music Heaven."

He was elected to the Nashville Songwriters Association Hall of Fame and to the Georgia Music Hall of Fame and was chosen (along with Hank Williams and Harlan Howard) one of the Three All-Time Greatest Country Music Songwriters by *Billboard* Magazine.

Bill was the first Country Music artist to host a network game show (ABC-TV's "The Better Sex"), has been an actor on ABC-TV's soap "One Life To Live" and has appeared on numerous TV variety and game shows. He has hosted several shows on TNN: The Nashville Network, including the popular game show "Fandango." He is a host of TNN's "Opry Backstage" show which precedes "The Grand Ole Opry Live." In 1990 he released another album, entitled *Yesteryear*, which also was the name of a radio show he hosted on The Nashville Network Radio.

His autobiography, *Whisperin' Bill*, was published in 1989 and now is in its fourth printing. Bill's latest literary work is the hilarious book, *I Hope You're Living As High On The Hog As The Pig You Turned Out To Be*, was published in 1993. Both books are by Longstreet Press.

Although work is something Bill has always thrived on, he acknowledges in the true country spirit: "I love what I do, and consider myself very blessed to have been able to create and perform music all these years. But what I truly enjoy more than anything else is the peace and quiet of home.

ERNIE ASHWORTH

Opry Staff Band members Billy Linneman, left, and Jimmy Capps listen attentively as Ernie explains his latest broadcasting venture while son, Mike, watches in the background.

It's a long way from the cotton fields of Huntsville, Alabama to the stage of the world famous Grand Ole Opry, but Ernie Ashworth has proved that with enough determination, ambition and hard work, it can be done. Ernie became an Opry fan at an early age and dreamed that someday he could become a part of this great show. He came to Nashville in the early fifties and joined a band as their vocalist doing night club work in the Nashville area. He always had a talent for writing songs and admits that he could write songs before he could play music.

Once he arrived in Nashville, he had the chance to play his songs for some of the music publishing companies and his songs were recorded by some of the top country artists including Carl Smith, Little Jimmy Dickens, Johnny Horton, Wilma Lee Cooper and others. During this time he met Wesley Rose who took Ernie under his wing and signed him as an exclusive writer for Acuff-Rose Publishing Company and recorded him on M.G.M. But recording success was to evade him at this time so, in 1957, Ernie went back to his home town of Huntsville, Alabama and started work at Redstone Arsenal in guided missile work.

In 1960 he was again contacted by Wesley Rose who told him Decca records wanted to record him and this time he was on his way. His first record, "Each Moment" went into the top 10 national charts. His next record, "You Can't Pick A Rose In December," was another top 10. He had two other top 20 records for Decca before changing to Hickory records, a label owned by Acuff-Rose. His string of top 10 records continued including "Everybody But Me," and "I Take The Chance." In 1963 came the smash hit he had been waiting for, "Talk Back Trembling Lips." This one went to #1 and stayed on the national charts for 36 weeks. It did quite well in the pop charts also. It was one of the nations first crossover records.

In March of 1964 Ernie saw his lifelong dream come true when he was invited to join the Grand Ole Opry. After this came more top 10 records, "A Week In The Country," "I Love to Dance With Annie," "The D.J. Cried," "At Ease Heart" and more. From 1960 to 1970 every record recorded by Ernie hit the national charts. Twelve of these were top 10. Quite an accomplishment for any artist.

Ernie now owns a Country Music radio station WSLV in Ardmore, Tennessee, and is always looking to purchase other broadcast properties. When someone asked Ernie what drew him to the entertainment field, he just smiled and said, "It's more fun than the cotton field."

When Clint Black accepted the Country Music Association's Horizon Award in 1989, he said, "I was standing on this stage here at the Grand Ole Opry, and I said this was like stepping into a picture I've been looking at all my life."

The RCA Records' artist had ties to the Opry long before he "stepped into the picture" and became its 66th member during the Jan. 10, 1991 taping of the Opry's 65th anniversary special on the CBS Television Network.

While watching a documentary on Minnie Pearl, a young Clint Black listened as she told how Opry founder George D. Hay, trying to calm the nervous young comedienne before her first appearance on the show, told her to "Just love 'em, honey, and they'll love you right back."

"I thought, 'What a great perspective. What a great thing to know,'" explained the singer/songwriter. "And whenever I was nervous and going out on the big stages for the first time, I thought of Minnie. And I thought of Judge Hay as if he were standing there giving me the same advice to calm me down."

Being nervous isn't what Black remembers most about his debut performance on the Opry stage on April 22, 1989 just a month after his first single "A Better Man" was released and one month before the release of his first album *Killin' Time*.

"I was in the middle of singing "Killin' Time" and I thought to myself, 'I can feel Hank Williams. I can feel Ernest Tubb.' And I found out after I got off stage that that was the centerpiece from the Ryman," he recalled and quickly added, "I got goose bumps just now thinking about it."

His first album generated five No. 1 singles "A Better Man," "Killin' Time," "Nobody's Home," "Walkin' Away" and "Nothing's News." He is the first artist in any field, including pop, to have five No. 1 singles off a debut album, according to *Radio & Records* Magazine.

The LP remained at No. 1 on the country charts for 28 weeks and went platinum. His follow up album, *Put Yourself in My Shoes*, has also gone platinum. It went to No. 1 and the title tune and the single "Loving Blind" from the LP are his sixth and seventh consecutive No. 1 singles. "One More Payment" is another Top 10 Hit. Clint's two albums: *The Hard Way* and *No Time To Kill* has elevated country lyrics to the level of poetry.

However, winning awards or selling a million

Clint Black tips his hat to the audience after being introduced as an Opry member by friend Garth Brooks.

albums don't equate to Opry membership for Black who described his induction as "an honor and a privilege" but something "removed from the business and entirely personal."

"I'm short of words. I've always had things to say and people to thank for my achievements and all but this is such a personal thing," he noted. "It's a lot like somebody asking me into their home. It's like when you build or buy a house and your neighbors ask you over. You've been accepted into your neighborhood."

Back in his Houston neighborhood, Black grew up listening to Country Music. He and his family—his father, G. A., his mother, Ann, his brothers, Mark, Brian and Kevin—watched "Hee Haw" on TV every weekend.

"My dad is a Country Music fanatic, lives and breathes it. My mother just loves music in general."

Still, Black said, he never dreamed of becoming a member of the Opry. "I don't know why. It wasn't from lack of want. It was just something that I thought happened to other people."

When it finally happened to him, Black realized that his mom and dad ought to be there for his induction and he flew his parents to Nashville from Houston for the anniversary show.

After his introduction as the Opry's newest family member, Black recalled his earlier comment at the CMA Awards and added, "The picture keeps getting better and better."

Garth receives an armful of roses from admiring Opry fans!

"What a dream to say, yeah, I not only play at the Grand Ole Opry, but I am a member of the Grand Ole Opry," said Garth Brooks two days after becoming the Opry's 65th member on Oct. 6, 1990, to initiate the Opry's 65th birthday celebration.

For the Oklahoma native, Grand Ole Opry membership marked the realization of a lifelong ambition and still was foremost in his thoughts the day of the 1990 Country Music Association Awards show. A first-time CMA nominee, he was the top contender with five nominations.

At the 1991 CMA Awards Show he won four awards: Entertainer of the Year; Album of the Year; Single of the Year; and Music Video of the Year.

The Capitol/Nashville artist took home two of those CMA awards, winning the prestigious Horizon Award for career achievement and the Video of the Year for the song "The Dance," which was a No. 1 hit for him for three straight weeks.

The youngest of six children, Garth was born in Tulsa but grew up in Yukon, an oil town near Oklahoma City. (His mother recorded for Capitol Records in the mid-1950s under the name Colleen Carroll and was a regular on Red Foley's Ozark Mountain Jubilee.)

His first move to Nashville in 1985 lasted only 23 hours before Garth returned home to complete a degree in advertising/marketing at Oklahoma State University.

In 1987 he returned to Nashville to pursue a career in music and within six months had signed with Capitol. His first single, "Much Too Young (To Feel This Damn Old)," went to No. 8 on the charts. The single was one of five songs he co-wrote on his debut album, *Garth Brooks*.

This self-titled LP made *Billboard's* Top 10 Country Albums chart and was certified platinum. It produced three No. 1 singles: "Not Counting You," "The Dance" and "If Tomorrow Never Comes," a Garth Brooks/Kent Blazy collaboration which won International Song of the Year honors from the Nashville Songwriters Association and the London-based Country Music People magazine.

His second album, *No Fences*, shipped gold and went double platinum. It went to No. 1 after only two weeks on *Billboard's* Country Albums chart.

The LP has produced two No. 1 hits: "Friends in Low Places," which shot to No. 1 after only eight weeks, and "Unanswered Prayers," which Garth co-wrote. His third single from the album, "Two of a Kind, Workin' on a Full-House," made the top five on the charts. His next album, *"Ropin' the Wind"* entered Billboard's Top-200 album charts at number one, the first time any album has ever done that.

When he became an Opry member, Garth said, "I have always been treated like family when I was at the Opry, but now to be recognized as a member is among the class of honors that will never be topped no matter how long or how far my career goes."

Just how far that career will take him remains a question mark, but for now, the Opry's "new traditionalist" stylist is riding high at the top of the Country Music world.

Jim Ed and his model/artist/dancer wife, Becky pack up and tour some of America's most popular and scenic travel destinations each week on TNN's "Going Our Way."

Over the past three decades, Jim Ed Brown, has firmly established himself in the minds of Country fans as a masterful presence in every aspect of the Country entertainment field.

The native of Sparkman, Arkansas was one of five children—two boys and three girls—of a struggling lumberman and his wife. Some of his earliest memories are of close, "family" times, when all the members of the household would gather on Saturday nights to listen to the Grand Ole Opry on a battery-powered radio. Jim Ed and his older sister, Maxine were fascinated by what they heard and soon began harmonizing together. A few years later Jim Ed and Maxine began to perform occasionally on local radio shows.

By Jim Ed's second year in college, he and Maxine were regular members of the "Barnyard Frolic" on KLRA in Little Rock, and together they had penned what was to become their first hit record, "Looking Back To See." They became members of The Louisiana Hayride and went on to join Red Foley as featured regulars on his Ozark Jubilee in 1955.

Later that year, younger sister Bonnie joined them and as "The Browns" they scored an immediate top-10 hit with "Here Today and Gone To-morrow." The group signed with RCA Victor in 1956, and two number-one releases followed in quick succession: "I Take The Chance" and "I Heard The Bluebird Sing."

Jim Ed's career took a vastly different turn when he was called to a two-year stint in the service. After his discharge he rejoined his sisters to record the song which would leave an indelible mark on musical history, "The Three Bells." Released in 1959, "The Three Bells" sold over a million copies and created a sensation as the first number-one country song ever to cross over to number-one on the pop and rhythm-and-blues charts, as well. Other classic hits, including "The Old Lamplighter" and "Scarlet Ribbons" soon followed.

By the mid-60's, however, the rigors of combining busy careers with caring for their growing families brought both Bonnie and Maxine to the decision to permanently retire from the group. Jim Ed was left to carry on alone, and in 1966 he scored his first solo success with "Pop-A-Top Again." Through the late 60's and early 70's he continued to grow as a star in his own right with more hit singles, including "Southern Loving," "Sometime Sunshine," and memorable "Morning." A six-season run as co-host of the syndicated weekly television series "Nashville On The Road" began in 1975, further enhancing Jim Ed's career and leading to his being selected as a national advertising spokesperson for Dollar General Stores.

Then in 1976, he teamed with Helen Cornelius to form one of the most successful recording duos of all time. With smash releases like "Don't Bother To Knock," "Fools," and the back-to-back number-ones, "I Don't Want To Have To Marry You," "Saying Hello, Saying I Love You, Saying Goodbye," and "Lying In Love With You."

In 1983, Jim Ed became the host of TNN's "You Can Be A Star," the Country Music talent hunt which aired daily on The Nashville Network. He is now paired with his beautiful wife, Becky, as co-hosts of TNN's popular travel show, "Going Our Way." Jim Ed joined the Grand Ole Opry in 1963.

If there is one word best-suited to describe Jim Ed Brown, it is versatile. As a dynamic component in duets and a trio, as a solo recording artist, and as a popular television host, in the course of his professional lifetime he has filled role after role with shining success.

Bill shares a joke backstage with his right-hand man, long-time friend, band member, songwriter and recording artist, George Riddle.

When it comes to country comedy hit records, Bill Carlisle has always hit the right spot at the right time. Like an archer with his bow drawn and ready, Bill has shot to the top in country humor with such records as "Too Old To Cut The Mustard," "What Kinda Deal Is This?" and "Poke Salat Annie."

The story behind Bill Carlisle demonstrates the endurance of a solid musical background, a family background that spirited Bill on his way to the top.

"When I was growing up, our family'd get together for a good old-fashioned sing-along every Sunday," recalls Bill. "We had quite a chorus with Mom, Dad, my four brothers, two sisters and me. Those were great days back in Wakefield, Kentucky, and I'm sure they had a lot to do with my becoming a musician and entertainer."

Indeed they did, for Bill never once ventured away from his want to be a country star. He continued singing at home, and then organized his own group, The Carlisles, and headed for the big time.

On his first big radio engagement in Cincinnati, Bill and The Carlisles recorded a song that brings memories to many country fans: "Rainbow At Midnight." That song was the initial success that started Bill and The Carlisles on their long, highly-successful journey into the Country Music spotlight.

"Knoxville was the Country Music center in the early '50s," explains the broad-grinning Bill, "so we packed up our show and moved from Ohio to Tennessee." The talented group joined such famed performers as Don Gibson, Chet Atkins, The Carter Family, Homer and Jethro, Carl Butler and Archie Campbell, and that is company enough to play to standing ovations for months on end.

Naturally, talent such as the Carlisles was not left unnoticed and, in 1953, Bill and his group received an invitation to join the Grand Ole Opry. "Too Old To Cut The Mustard" and "What Kinda Deal Is This?," "No Help Wanted" and "Poke Salat Annie" have been such tremendous hits that numerous other artists have recorded them.

Some artists kick one foot up as they finish a song, some throw their guitar to their side, some wiggle, some bend way over their mike, and then there is Bill—he jumps. "I just do it, always have," Bill replies candidly.

Still, "jumping" is not the only adjective to pounce upon this beloved country star. Wise would be another. Bill was wise enough when he began his career to know that comic songs were his bag of tricks, and he has never disappointed his fans.

Another adjective for Bill Carlisle is enduring. His style, his manner, his personal touch in Country Music have carried on steadily through the years.

The Carlisles consist of his son Billy and George Riddle, plus, the "best undiscovered country singer in the world," Marshal Barnes, who plays bass fiddle for the group.

Bill and his crew have been crowd pleasers for over 40 years and no doubt will remain favorites for years to come.

Opry President Hal Durham and Roy Clark join hands prior to cutting and sampling the large cake backstage at the Opry.

Roy Clark is the consummate entertainer and showman.

Roy's a virtuoso of all stringed instruments, and also plays the trombone, trumpet and piano. Whether singing simple love ballads or rowdy country rockers, Roy brings audiences to their feet around the world. Musical talent combined with a quick wit and an impish smile is the recipe for one of American music's best entertainers.

Roy has headlined at some of the world's most prestigious venues, from Carnegie Hall and Madison Square Garden in New York to the Grand Palace in Brussels, and the impressive Rossiya Theatre in Moscow. He is recognized as one of the top five draws for fairs and rodeos and has headlined state fairs in most of the 50 states.

His acting debut in the mid-60s on "The Beverly Hillbillies" spawned several successful acting roles on television and in movies. A frequent guest on major talk and variety shows, Roy was the first Country Music artist to guest host Johnny Carson's "Tonight Show." His overall attractiveness as a performer has landed him jobs hosting his own series of television specials. And, he has been the host of the ever-popular "Hee Haw" show for over two decades.

Roy's achievements have not gone unnoticed. A partial list of his most prestigious awards are "Entertainer of the Year" from the Academy of Country Music and the Country Music Association, "Comedy Act of the Year" by the Academy of Country Music, "Picker of the Year" in Playboy Magazine's Reader's Poll, "Best Country Guitarist" from Guitar Magazine, the Country Music Banjo Championship, and the list continues. In 1982, he received a Grammy for his performance of "Alabama Jubilee." Roy became a Grand Ole Opry member in 1987.

Roy Clark takes his artistry one step beyond most entertainment boundaries. With the belief that music can bridge continents, he takes his message of goodwill to other peoples of the world.

In 1976, Roy led his own show to the Soviet Union. That record-breaking tour sold out 18 concerts in Moscow, Leningrad and Riga.

Most of Roy's philanthropic generosity goes unheralded, but he is always available to lend his time and talents to a worthwhile cause. His major interest is in helping young people. The annual Roy Clark Charity Golf Tournament in Tulsa has raised over one million for the city's Children's Medical Center.

Over the years, Roy has recorded a string of hits both vocally and instrumentally. Perhaps he is best associated with his hit version of "Yesterday, When I Was Young" and his own 12-string guitar version of "Malaguena."

But, it's as a total entertainer where Roy shines. His good friend Minnie Pearl observed: "Roy is the original Peck's Bad Boy! He's still the same impish, mischievous little boy that he was when he was growing up in Virginia. He is truly one of our most talented entertainers. I love working with him—I love him."

Opry General Manager, Bob Whittakaer, left, Opry President Hal Durham, and Jerry's personal manager, Tandy Rice, right, help Jerry celebrate his 20th Opry Anniversary backstage.

I am convinced that there is only one place where there is no laughter and that's Hell. I have made arrangements to miss Hell, 'Praise God,' I won't ever have to be anywhere that there ain't no laughter."

Jerry Clower is his real name. The stories he tells really happened. The laughter that greets these stories is the real thing. Not canned. Jerry Clower is a humorist with albums which tickle the nation's funnybone. He's made guest appearances on top shows in television and radio, and requests pour in for engagements as speaker and professional entertainer. But there's more. Listening to Jerry is not merely listening, because Jerry does more than tell a story funny: he carries his audience along with him, on that coon hunt or whatever. The locale may be regional, but the humor is universal.

What is it that makes Jerry a good entertainer? What it is can be seen surfacing in his background: His mother says that he was always talking. It's as natural for Jerry to tell a story as it is for a politician to make a promise. And Jerry is not delivering material conjured up by a staff of writers. The basic part of every story is, to quote him, "something real that has happened to me or almost happened!"

Jerry's growing up was typical of country boys all over America. He loved sports; and, with his friends, sat glued to the battery radio listening to ballgames. His favorite food was french fries with molasses, but home-raised groceries included hog meat, biscuits, chicken, sweet potatoes, and don't knock it if you've never played tackle in the line.

The fertile imagination received early cultivation: Jerry and his friends were resourceful at developing their own entertainment. A Saturday afternoon when they were not working would find them in the pasture having a rodeo, which meant rounding up a bunch of calves and riding them. Or down at the creek playing 'gator. Or Tarzan. Or they might go coon or rabbit hunting.

In addition to the staggering number of speaking engagements, guest spots include: The David Frost Show, the Charley Pride personal appearances, Mike Douglas Show, Country Crossroads Radio Show, the Bill Anderson and Wilburn Brothers TV Shows, and as a regular member of the Grand Ole Opry in 1973. Jerry has sold millions of record albums, has taped radio and television commercials, both local and national; and his apt ad libs are the joy of all talk show hosts. He has written three books: "Ain't God Good!," "Let the Hammer Down," and "Life Ever Laughter." He has been named "Country Comic of the Year" for nine consecutive years by the major country music publications.

Jerry's show business career is based on one thing, being natural, being himself. Roy Clark has remarked, "he brought back some memories that I cherish, but I was about to forget them." Jerry Clower sells the really good life—laughter, remembering the fun you've had, the friends, the simple things you enjoyed, the humorous side of even the bad times.

John—with his rose colored glasses perched on top of his head—lends his own special sound and styling to one of his many hit songs.

John Conlee, Country Music's banner-carrier for the common man, lives the life of which he sings.

"There are more of us ordinary folks than anybody else," says the entertainer who extolls the virtues—and hardships—of everyday, middle-class life in hit songs like "Common Man," "Working Man," and "Friday Night Blues."

"I spend all my off-time, what I have of it, with my family on our farm," he explains. "I enjoy it. There's no glamour to it. Woodworking, gunsmithing or driving a tractor require getting grease or varnish all over you. It's dirty work, but I like it."

John Conlee speaks passionately about the family farm. Reared on a 250-acre Kentucky farm, he had raised hogs, cultivated tobacco with mules, and mowed pastures with tractors before moving on to become a funeral home attendant, then a pop music disc jockey at a Nashville radio station and finally—pretty suddenly in the mid-1970s—a rising country star.

John was instrumental in the crusade on behalf of America's farmers that mushroomed into the massive FarmAid concert events. Through his efforts the Family Farm Defense Fund was created and John helped organize and participated in the FarmAid concerts that assisted troubled farmers.

With John Conlee, we have a sincere and sensitive man who can translate lyrics into feelings as well as anyone. John is also an accomplished songwriter having penned two of his biggest hits: the country standard: "Rose Colored Glasses," and "Backside of Thirty." Other chart busters include: "Lady Lay Down," "I'm Only In It For The Love," "In My Eyes," "The Carpenter," "Domestic Life," "I Don't Remember Loving You," "Busted," and "Mama's Rockin' Chair." His riveting live performance of Micky Newbury's "American Trilogy" always holds concert audiences spellbound.

John received an RIAA Gold Record for his "Greatest Hits Volume I" album, an awards from the Academy of Country Music, Billboard, Cashbox and Music City News magazines, and Broadcast Music, Inc. (BMI). He became a member of the Grand Ole Opry in February 1981.

Both a distinctive vocalist and discriminating song judge, John views his music in this manner. "My personal preference would be for music to get to the place where we don't have to have labels. I don't think they're important. It's either good music or it's not. I just want to be thought of as a good communicator of music."

For all his acclaim as one of Country Music's most distinctive song stylists, he eschews show biz glitz for a simpler, more down-to-earth lifestyle. As he puts it, what you see with John Conlee is exactly what you get.

An early family photo shows the late Stoney Cooper and Wilma Lee with daughter Carol Lee in the middle. She now leads the Carol Lee Singers, the quartet that accompanies the Opry members and guests with backup vocals.

Wilma Lee Cooper is just now approaching the pinnacle of her musical career. A featured member of the Grand Ole Opry cast since 1957, Wilma Lee is one of it's most respected artists. She and her Clinch Mountain Clan are the finest practitioners of authentic traditional mountain music.

Wilma Leigh Leary grew up in the wild and beautiful mountains of West Virginia. Her marriage to Dale T. Cooper created a team that was to make an important place for itself in the history of Country Music. "Wilma Lee & Stoney Cooper and The Clinch Mountain Clan" recorded for Columbia Records such classics as "Tramp On The Street," "Walking My Lord Up Calvary's Hill" and "The Legend Of The Dogwood Tree." Successful chart records on the Hickory label followed, including "Come Walk With Me," "Big Midnight Special" and "There's A Big Wheel."

"I sing just like I did back when I was growing up in those West Virginia mountains. I've never changed. I can't change. I couldn't sing any other way," she says. "I would say my style is just the old mountain style of singing. I am traditional country. I'm a country singer with the mountain whang to it." She notes that she sings a lot of story songs, and if listeners don't understand the words to that type of song they miss the story. "So, when I sing, I try to speak my words as plainly as I can, so folks will know what I am saying." Wilma Lee's work is being preserved in the Library of Congress and the Smithsonian Institution.

Country Music has no better trouper than Wilma Lee Cooper. Through the years she's worked virtually every important regular Saturday night radio-stage presentation in the country and she remembers fondly the days of traveling two lane highways between one night stands, sometimes with very little sleep. Her "dues" are paid in full.

Following "Stoney's" death on March 22, 1977, Wilma Lee assembled a talented group of young musicians to comprise "The Clinch Mountain Clan." She exhibits intense pride in their character and integrity as well as in their musicianship and never fails to introduce them on a show by name, adding emphatically, "I'm proud of every one of 'em!"

As the first and foremost lady in Bluegrass Music, Wilma Lee is a rarity in a practically all male form of music. But hardly so rare and so unique as her powerful, clear and true singing voice, backed by her big D-45 Martin Guitar, the fiddle, five string banjo, dobro guitar and bass. The fascinated promoter of an outdoor Bluegrass Music festival, listening to her performance over the large sound system, summed up his assessment in a few words, "she's a thoroughbred."

Wilma Lee Cooper is indeed a "thoroughbred" and her music is fully as authoritative and original as is her voice. Alternately sad, happy and plaintive, her songs seem to suggest the clean mountain air, the rugged slopes and lush meadows of the best of West Virginia.

On a cold, snowy night in December on the thirtieth day, in the little town of Dry Ridge, Kentucky . . . a Star was born. She was the first of seven children to be born to William and Sarah Penick. They named her Mary Frances, but she was destined to become Skeeter Davis, one of the most successful female entertainers in the history of Country Music.

Skeeter's professional career began when she and her best friend, Betty Jack Davis, started singing as the Davis Sisters on a local television program while in their last year of high school. Soon after they graduated, they took their first airplane trip to New York City, where they met the Chief of A & R, Steve Sholes at RCA Victor Records and got a recording contract! They recorded the song, "I Forgot More Than You'll Ever Know" and their record sold a million copies and became a Gold Standard.

Their immediate success was overshadowed by a terrible, tragic accident on August 2, 1953. A soldier had fallen asleep at the wheel and his car struck the car carrying the Davis Sisters. Betty Jack lost her life and Skeeter was left critically hurt, physically and emotionally. After awhile, she was persuaded to sing and record with Betty Jack's sister, Georgia. They had some successful records and toured with Grand Ole Opry stars, Carl Smith, Hank Snow, Mother Maybell, the Carter Sisters and they even toured with Elvis Presley before Georgia retired to raise her family.

Skeeter started her solo career in 1958 with Chet Atkins producing her records. He had always been there from the start, playing guitar. Now she was one of the first he was to produce. She was named "Most Promising Female Vocalist" of the year and had her first top ten record, "Set Him Free" in 1959. She also got her first grammy nomination for that record and her dreams came true when she was asked to join the Grand Ole Opry in August 1959. Skeeter had several top ten records in the C & W Charts before she crossed over into the pop charts with "My Last Date With You." She collaborated with Boudeliaux Bryant on the lyrics to Floyd Cramer's beautiful melody. This opened new doors for her. She was on Dick Clark's American Bandstand several times and did shows with Connie Francis, Bobby Vinton, Beach

Skeeter playfully serves pieces of the giant Grand Ole Opry Birthday cake to a hungry Opry Crowd.

Boys, Righteous Brothers and even the Rolling Stones. Skeeter and Chet found a song called "The End Of The World" and it went to be number one on the pop charts and became a top ten record in almost every country. She has Gold Records from South Africa, Silver Records from Norway and, of course, the United States as well as many awards from all the trade magazines and jukebox operators such as Best Record Of The Year, Top Female Vocalist Of The Year, and Entertainer Of The Year.

Skeeter has performed in England, Germany, Japan, Holland, Sweden, Norway, Ireland, Denmark, Finland, New Zealand, Virgin Islands, Singapore and Malaysia. In 1983, Skeeter was at the big Music Festival in Jamaica with Aretha Franklin, Beach Boys, Grateful Dead, Gladys Knight and the Pips, Joe Jackson, Peter Tosh, Rita Marley and others. She was booked on the show because the promoter found out she was the Jamaicans favorite artist.

She has an album recorded with NRBQ (New Rhythm & Blues Quartet) and her autobiography "Bus Fare to Kentucky" is now a best seller. Skeeter is a "country" girl from Dry Ridge, Kentucky who has sung in every "big city" in every state with the exception of Alaska, and plans to keep on singing. Maybe Alaska will be her next stop.

Little Jimmy welcomes another legendary entertainer, Bob Hope, to the Opry Stage.

When Jimmy Dickens was in his teens, he decided coal mining wasn't for him. It was a wise decision for Jimmy and a lucky one for his millions of fans. It is rare that a Country Music artist retains top popularity decade after decade such as Little Jimmy Dickens. Jimmy, the oldest member of a family of 13 children was born in Bolt, West Virginia. His initial start in radio was at a local radio station WOLS, at Beckley, West Virginia, where he opened the station's program "crowing like a rooster." Though he had to walk to and from the station, he loved being in radio, and set his aim for the entertainment field.

After winning local acclaim, he moved to such other places as WIBC in Indianapolis and WLW in Cincinnati. Roy Acuff introduced Little Jimmy to the Grand Ole Opry in 1948 and he continues today being one of the most dynamic entertainers on the weekly W.S.M. radio show.

Shortly after joining the Opry, Jimmy joined the ranks of Hank Williams, Lefty Frizzell and Eddy Arnold in releasing hit after hit on Columbia Records. All remember hits like "A-Sleepin' At The Foot Of The Bed," "Take An Old Cold Tater," "Out Behind The Barn," "Little, But I'm Loud," "Country Boy," "Wabash Cannonball," as well as dozens of others.

Jimmy became a regular on the popular TV show, "Stars of the Grand Ole Opry" shown around the world, and continues to be shown today as "Country Classic." He was a regular on the "Phillip Morris T.V. Show" for 18 months before resigning to entertain abroad, which resulted in 13 trips to Europe, 3 trips to Southeast Asia, and twice to Vietnam, where he entertained troops under fire.

During the spring of 1964, Jimmy became the first Country Music artist to completely circle the globe on a world tour. That same year, after many years of worldwide popularity in the Country Music field, he won a place in the Pop Music spotlight with his recording of "May The Bird Of Paradise Fly Up Your Nose." At this point in his career, he found himself on all national network shows. He continued to retain his popularity by releasing hits such as "We Could," "Life Turned Her That Way," "Raggedy Ann," "Preacher Man," etc. In 1989 Rounder Records began marketing his 1949-1955 hits on a new LP titled "Straight From The Heart." He reportedly works more dates than any other artist on the Grand Ole Opry year after year.

When he is not working, Jimmy and his beautiful wife, Mona, enjoy the quiet life of their Brentwood home just south of Nashville.

Little Jimmy Dickens greatest moment came at the Country Music Association Award Show in 1983 when he was inducted by his peers into the Country Music Hall of Fame.

Although only 4 feet, 11 inches tall, his peers refer to Jimmy as the "TATER-The Littlest, but the Biggest Star At The Opry." This is illustrated by the constant flash-bulbs throughout the Opry House when his small frame with the giant voice appears each weekend at the Grand Ole Opry.

With his unassuming style and personality, Joe Diffie could be the boy-next-door or just a regular Joe, but his talent and number one hits tell a different story.

This Duncan, Oklahoma, native grew up in a musical family. His Dad played guitar and his Mother sang. As a child Joe recalls riding in the family pickup and singing "You Are My Sunshine," "Peace In The Valley" and "Amazing Grace."

He also remembers listening to his Dad's record collection. "My Dad had a huge record collection. His favorites were all country — George Jones, Merle Haggard, Johnny Cash, Lefty Frizzell. They were my favorites, too. When I got a little older, I was one of those guys who knew every dad-gum song on the radio and would run people crazy singing them all," Joe laughs. "I'd sing 'em all, whether they were men's or women's songs. I didn't have any idea how good I was, but I could always match their licks. It was almost like I couldn't help it," he shakes his head. "It was like an obsession with me.

"Once my Dad and I were listening to a George Jones record, and he said, 'Ain't nobody can sing like he can,' and I thought, 'I can.'" Today, years later, Joe is singing, if not like Gorge Jones, then in his own inimitable style. And, it looks as if that style fits him perfectly, because Joe's songs keep heading in the right direction: to the top.

At different times in Duncan, Joe worked on an oil-drilling rig and in an iron foundry while pursuing his singing career in local honky-tonks and clubs. He joined a gospel group called Higher Purpose, then later hooked up with a bluegrass band called Special Edition. "Back in those days, I'd often have people tell me that I oughta go to Nashville," Joe recalls. "I'd just think to myself, 'Yeah, sure! Right!'

Then in 1986, the foundry shut down and Joe was unemployed. This prompted him to borrow some money from his parents and move to Nashville. He worked in the Gibson Guitar warehouse and sang demo-tapes of songs which became hits for other artists: Alabama, Billy Dean, Ricky Van Shelton, and Keith Whitley, to name a few. As a staff songwriter for Forest Hills Music, in 1989, he co-wrote Holly Dunn's No. 4 hit, "There Goes My Heart Again."

Joe's demo singing landed him a recording contract in 1990, and his first album: "A Thousand Winding Roads" produced four No. 1 hits;

Just a "Regular Joe" with a "Honky Tonk attitude."

"Home," "If The Devil Danced (In Empty Pockets)," "If You Want Me To," and "New Way To Light Up An Old Flame," both of which he co-wrote.

Joe enjoyed another No. 1 hit with "Ships That Don't Come In" from his 1992 "Regular Joe" album. That album also yielded the Top 10 hit singles, "Is It Cold In Here," one of four songs he wrote, and "Startin' Over Blues." Hits from his album, "Honky Tonk Attitude," include the title cut, and "Prop Me Up Beside The Jukebox," and "John Deere Green."

On November 27, 1993, Joe joined the Grand Ole Opry cast. "It's such a thrill to perform on the Grand Ole Opry, and think that a lot of history has gone down there. It's the only place where I still get nervous, and still get cotton mouth," he remarked.

"As a little boy I used to listen to the Opry on the radio and dream of belonging. All other achievements pale in comparison and for the first time I feel like I really belong to the Country Music family.

"I'm so overwhelmed with the emotion of that little boy's dream becoming a reality, I don't know how I feel…joy…pride…gratitude…all mixed up together. This means more to me than words can express. The Opry is a major institution, and I think it's pretty cool," he added.

And Opry fans everywhere are happy that this "Regular Joe" with a "Honky Tonk Attitude" realized his boyhood dream.

Roy graciously visits with fans and signs autographs backstage during the Opry show.

From the time he was five years old, Roy Drusky dreamed of becoming a professional baseball player. "I ate, slept and breathed baseball," he admits. But baseball was not to be a part of his professional life. The switch did not occur because of lack of talent—he was offered a tryout with the Cleveland Indians—but because music became the dominating factor in Roy's life.

If anyone had asked Roy's mother about her son's ambition when he was still a youngster, chances are she would never have answered "music." Mrs. Drusky was a church pianist for twenty years and, of course, it was a natural thing for her to want Roy to obtain some musical training. However, baseball practice and piano lessons were not compatible, and the result was that the piano never held any appeal for him. Singing was a different matter. The Young People's Choir at the Moreland Baptist Church offered Roy the opportunity to express his musical ability and yet allowed plenty of time for athletics. No one realized, then, including Roy, that his church singing would be laying the foundation for a career later in life.

Music took over Roy's life once he began performing regularly over WEAS Radio in Decatur, Georgia. There was no doubt in Roy's mind but what music should be his occupation. He was offered and accepted a job announcing on WEAS in addition to performing. Soon he added two weekly television shows in Atlanta to his activities and many "live" shows all around that section of the country. He was contacted by Radio Station KEVE in Minneapolis with an offer to work at the station and to perform regularly at one of the top clubs in the country. Though he regretted having to leave his hometown, Roy felt the offer was too good too good to refuse and was soon on his way to the far north. "My time in Minneapolis proved to be both pleasant and invaluable," says Roy. "I didn't realize what devoted country fans those

people were in the upper Midwest. I got a boost to my career and my ego during my eighteen-month stay."

Songwriting, as well as singing, was the eventual cause that brought Roy to Nashville. While working in Minnesota he had made several trips to Music City to record. Finally he got the break he needed with "Alone With You," which jumped into hit territory. Faron Young, who was on the Capitol label at the time, was also having good luck with the song at the same time. Realizing that he must take advantage of the success generated by his song, Roy moved to Nashville where he could have the opportunity of employing all his talents. After a relatively brief period of time, the Grand Ole Opry beckoned him in 1958 and Roy's name went on the roster of the world's most renowned Country Music show. Roy has had over 50 chart records—10 of which were Number One. He has over 35 albums to his credit and over two dozen music awards.

Today, Roy's focus is on recording country/southern gospel albums. He has six to his credit, and is immensely popular performing gospel concerts around the country.

Holly entertains the Opry fans with one of her many hit songs.

Holly Dunn's first remembrance of the Grand Ole Opry was as a 2- or 3-year-old going to the Municipal Auditorium in San Antonio, Texas, and seeing Opry stars on tour.

The San Antonio native fell in love with country music and the Opry and made numerous guest appearances on the Opry before becoming a member of the radio show's cast on Oct. 14, 1989.

Holly burst upon the Country Music scene in the mid-1980s. She was named the Academy of Country Music's Top New Female Vocalist in 1986 and won the Country Music Association's Horizon Award in 1987.

In addition, she garnered three Grammy nominations and won the 1987 Nashville Songwriters Association's International Award for "Daddy's Hands." Her songwriting talents earned her the 1988 BMI Country songwriter of the Year Award.

Holly's love of Country Music had prompted a move to Nashville two weeks after graduation from Abilene Christian University in Texas. She worked as a staff songwriter for four years before signing with MTM Records to pursue a singing career.

Over the next three years she recorded three top-selling albums for MTM: *Holly Dunn, Cornerstone* and *Across the Rio Grande,* which she and brother, Chris Waters, co-produced.

Her version of "Daddy's Hands," originally written as a Father's Day gift, stayed in the Top 10 for six months and earned two of her Grammy nominations.

Other hits followed, including "Only When I Love" and "Love Someone Like Me," which both went No. 1, along with "Strangers Again," "That's What Your Love Does To Me" and "Someday."

After MTM Records was sold, she signed with Warner Bros. Records in February 1989 and she and Waters co-produced her first album for the label, *The Blue Rose of Texas.* The sister/brother duo and Tom Shapiro co-wrote her first single from the LP, "Are You Ever Gonna Love Me," which became a No. 1 hit. Another hit single, "There Goes My Heart Again" soon followed.

Her recording of "A Face In The Crowd" with labelmate Michael Martin Murphey earned Grammy and CMA nominations for the duet. Holly recorded a second duet, "Maybe," with Kenny Rogers in 1989.

Her second Warner Bros. LP, *Heart Full of Love,* produced the hits "My Anniversary For Being A Fool," "You Really Had Me Going" and "Heart Full of Love." Her third album in 1992 was *"Getting It Dunn."*

Singer, songwriter, producer Holly Dunn is another younger generation country artist who has found a home at the Grand Ole Opry.

The 4 Guys held an Opry homecoming aboard the M/S Caribe on a recent Caribbean cruise. On deck are, left to right, John Frost, Laddie Cain; Opry stage manager, Tim Thompson, Sam Wellington; Opry stage hand, Tyler Bryan, and Brent Burkett.

Who says you have to stockpile a string of hit records and travel the nation's interstate system in a fleet of new silver-eagle buses to call yourself a success in the music business? There are many ways of looking at success, relative to your position on the highly scrutinized "Show-Biz" ladder. The 4 Guys choose to look at success as a journey rather than a destination.

Since their professional start on WWVA's "Jamboree U.S.A." in Wheeling, WV, "The Guys" have had numerous successes. Most important of which was an invitation from the Grand Ole Opry to join it's family of stars in Nashville, thereby becoming the first group in the history of that world famous show to be awarded regular membership without a list of "Hit Records." Fact is, The 4 Guys didn't even have a recording contract at the time. After joining The Opry in 1967, it wasn't long before "The Guys" became regulars in the main showrooms of the most prestigious hotels in Las Vegas, Reno & Lake Tahoe, Nevada, appearing on their own and with their long-time friend, Jimmy Dean. Their first major recording deal came later with Mercury Records, along with a two-year stint touring throughout the United States and Canada with Hank Williams, Jr.

Successes continued to mount as "The Guys" were invited to play most of this country's major theme parks, including: Disneyland, Six Flags over Texas, and Opryland U.S.A., where they were featured in their own show four consecutive years. Countless state and county fairs have also been added to their list of performance credits. They are certainly no strangers to television, appearing on many major network shows with the likes of Bob Hope, Dinah Shore, Willie Nelson, Dolly Parton & Merv Griffin. Most recently The 4 Guys have taken their harmony aboard cruise liners on the high seas.

The 4 Guys say their Opry Membership is their most valued achievement. High on the list also, is their long-time association with The Charley Pride Show, which featured "The Guys" and a then up and coming singer named Ronnie Milsap.

Whether it's success in a private enterprise, (The Guys owned and operated their highly popular Harmony House Theatre-Restaurant in Nashville for nearly 10 years), or whether it's successful careers on the Stage, Radio & Television, "The Guys," by any measure, are enjoying a very successful journey. Though the group has evolved through several personnel changes over the years, original members Sam Wellington & Brent Burkett, and long-time members John Frost & Laddie Cain have refused to sacrifice the dedication to quality and excellence platform on which The 4 Guys were founded.

If that so called "Big Record" never happens for them "The Guys" successful journey is sure to continue in one or more of their many other Show-Biz Arenas. Meanwhile, their fame grows on and on as each year they win millions of new fans and friends!

LARRY GATLIN & THE GATLIN BROTHERS

Steve, Larry and Rudy Gatlin share a funny story backstage at the Opry with their good friend, Charley Pride.

The three-star appeal of the Gatlins was born and nurtured in the Lone Star state. And it was in a west Texas setting that the inherent trait of singing harmony came as naturally as Texas beef. Those initial vocals had nothing to do with country, however, it was gospel that gave this Texas triad their first public performance. It was Mrs. Billie Gatlin who rather reluctantly let the irascible Rudy, 2, and Steve, 4, join their big brother Larry, 6, in a talent show at Hardin-Simmons University in Abilene in 1954. After the show, Mrs. Gatlin put her firstplace boys to bed knowing a talent had been awakened that would never sleep again.

"We didn't exactly have your normal childhood, but we did have ourselves a heck of a lot of fun with the music," Larry commented. "And come to think of it, the only thing that's really changed is that Rudy doesn't chase quarters across the stage anymore." (During live TV appearances as kids, members of the crew would roll coins across the studio floor and Rudy would inevitably run after them.)

The Gatlins didn't make the smooth Jackson Five-type transition from childhood to manhood performers without missing a beat. Instead, they took a rather circuitous route before landing back on their musical feet in the late '70s. Larry, after playing football at the University of Houston, flirted with the idea of becoming a lawyer.

"I taught fifth grade for a while, and I enjoyed it, but I knew it was temporary because my heart was in music," Steve said in reference to one of his background experiences before joining with the brothers on a full-time basis. Rudy says he relates to that. He periodically taught junior high

school math and history after graduating behind Steve at Texas Tech, but he knew all along he wanted an entertainment career.

Eventually, the music took precedence over all else, and the consummate songwriter/performer Larry Gatlin got his break by going West—Dottie West, that is. She was the one who took some of Larry's songs and offered to underwrite his move to Music City to get started as a scribe in the big time. The trek had begun for the Gatlins. Subsequently, Steve and Rudy (as well as sister LaDonna) followed Larry's lead and moved from Texas to Tennessee and were fortunate enough to make their first Nashville inroads by working with country music's First Lady, Tammy Wynette.

For the Gatlins, though, it was their music and no one else's which was most important. With that ever-present theme, the brothers put to track a song that took Larry all of 15 minutes to write. And it didn't take much more than that for the song, "Broken Lady," to hit #1 and earn a Grammy in 1976. The Gatlins had finally hit paydirt and they would go on to find the motherlode with "All The Gold In California" in 1979. They joined the Grand Ole Opry in 1976.

Larry explains that it was all due to one simple credo: "If we take care of our music the music will take care of us. It's not that we don't care about other people's music, it's just that nobody knows the Gatlins like the Gatlins, and nothing makes us happier than recording and performing our own material," he summed up.

Of course, the music has taken care of the Gatlins, with a pocketful of gold and #1 records, a collage of awards, enviable TV guestings and sold-out personal appearances.

DON GIBSON

*Don entertains the Opry audience
with one of his many hit songs.*

When considering great Country Music talents, Don Gibson's name has to be high on the list. As a songwriter/artist, Don has composed such classic standards as "Oh, Lonesome Me" and "I Can't Stop Loving You." More than 150 artists have recorded the later classic (Elvis Presley three times, for example) and Don's dividends from the song even include a gold record for the Ray Charles version.

Don knew he had something special the day he composed "I Can't Stop Loving You." He thought less of "Oh, Lonesome Me," written the same afternoon. "I thought it was nothing at all, so I sent it to Nashville and said, 'Give it to George Jones. It might make him a good number.' I had no idea I'd ever cut it, but Chet Atkins and Wesley Rose said that was the one they wanted me to record. I said, 'I don't want to do that junk. I thought you'd give it to George.' Well they insisted, so I said, 'I'll do it if you let me put 'I Can't Stop Loving You' on the back. I think it's the best song.' They didn't want to. Then they said they would but they weren't going to push it, and they didn't."

And to prove that it wasn't a fluke, Gibson also wrote "Blue Blue Day," "Legend In My Time," "Sweet Dreams," "Too Soon To Know," "Guess Away The Blues," "Country Green," "Who Cares," and scores of others. Yet you can't separate Don Gibson the songwriter and Don Gibson the singer and musician.

As a teenager he worked at a variety of jobs, in the textile mills in his native North Carolina, "hopping curbs and even delivering baby diapers," he recalled. And all to make enough money to finance his efforts to be an entertainer and songwriter. Don's father was a railroad man and there were three brothers and two sisters, so at an early age Don was on his own.

He was still a youngster when he moved to Knoxville to perform on the WNOX "Tennessee Barndance" and "Midday Merry-Go-Round." He soon organized his first band and a busy schedule of one-nighters and club dates in the area followed. And then he met Wesley Rose, president of Acuff-Rose Publications in Nashville. Rose heard some of Don's songs and sought him out. And just as Rose's father, Fred, discovered Hank Williams, Wesley discovered Don Gibson.

Don signed a song writing contract with Rose and a recording contract with RCA Victor followed in short order. His first single was "Too Soon To Know," and it was a good recording. But the second one was the smash hit. It was "Oh, Lonesome Me," which swept every major award in the country music field in 1958. During this period, Don joined The Grand Ole Opry as a regular. He rejoined the Opry in 1975.

But the nicest thing that ever happened to him, in his own words, "is her," his wife, Bobbi; a beautiful, charming girl from his home town, Shelby, N.C.

With all his many successes—including one movie, "From Nashville With Music"—what goals are there left for this giant of the Country Music industry? Don Gibson stops to think a moment when asked that sort of question. "To top myself," he will answer, finally. "I'd like to write another hit as big or bigger than, 'I Can't Stop Loving You,' and I think I can do it, too."

Vince Gill has finally achieved the success that his talent deserves. His career-breaking #1 single, "When I Call Your Name," won the multi-talented country singer/songwriter/guitarist a Grammy for Best Country Vocal Performance (Male), and the CMA Award for Single of the Year, and Male Vocalist of the Year. The title cut from his first MCA album also won him a host of other accolades, including five Academy of Country Music Award nominations, the Songwriter/Artist Award from the Nashville Songwriter Association, and six TNN Music City News Awards nominations. In August 1991 he joined the Grand Ole Opry and was CMA's Entertainer of the Year for 1993.

Even before his arrival in Nashville in 1984, Vince Gill was well-known as one of the most talented individuals in the music business. Not raw talent, either, but refined. He is blessed with a pure tenor voice and a riveting, pitch-perfect delivery. He's a studio-quality guitarist whose style is fiery but still tasteful. When he's not working on his own records, he's in great demand as a musician and singer for other artists' projects. His songs are passionate and heartfelt.

Vince grew up in Oklahoma playing bluegrass music. His first instruments were a four-string tenor guitar and his dad's banjo. In high school, he made a name for himself in bluegrass circles as a member of Mountain Smoke. The summer after high school, Gill was seriously considering a career as a professional golfer when a call came from Louisville, Kentucky. He threw all his belongings into his van and went off to join the Bluegrass Alliance, a progressive bluegrass group whose members at that time included Sam Bush and Dan Crary.

Vince could easily have accepted a career as a session singer and musician, but he continued to concentrate on writing songs and working toward a solo career. More important than a display of talent was the long overdue recognition by Country Music fans. "Never Alone," which he co-wrote with Rosanne Cash, was the first single and it made the Top 20. "Oklahoma Swing," a duet with Reba McEntire, made the Top 10. "When I Call Your Name," which featured Patty Loveless on harmonies, went all the way to #1 and won a CMA Award for Single of the Year as well as a Grammy for Best Country Vocal Performance, Male. The fourth hit from the album, "Never

Ralph Emery looks on in awe as Vince Gill drives one long and straight down the fairway.

Knew Lonely," went to #3. The album went gold (over 800,000 copies sold), which was better than his previous four albums combined.

To Vince, the radio and sales success was mirrored in the reaction of those who came to see him live. "About the time 'When I Call Your Name' started flying and doing great things, we pulled into this honky tonk where we were booked," he recalled. "We couldn't find a parking place. It was that way from the summer on. Everywhere we went there was a big crowd. There were times we'd kick off 'When I Call Your Name,' and the emotion that came from the crowd was frightening. There was one place in West Virginia, with about 6,000 people there, I got so moved it was hard to sing. It was wild."

Vince's road schedule intensified along with every other aspect of his career, but he's not complaining. "Now the music's speaking for itself. It's a great feeling."

Billy and wife, Ruth, have been a happily married couple for 50 years.

Success did not come easy for the son of a farmer and coal miner who was one of 13 children on a farm in Illinois. And it couldn't happen to a nicer guy. Billy's quiet but confident manner, whether it be a radio, TV or stage performance, is a refreshing experience.

Billy was born at Benton, Ill., and spent the most memorable part of his childhood fishing on a trot line in the Wabash River, where he dreamed of becoming a mechanical engineer. But he had developed a love for the guitar early in life.

"Daddy played the fiddle—or violin if you like—and we entertained at all the social functions around home," Billy says. "We were poor, but everybody else was too. I had one good pair of bib overalls which I scrubbed on the old rub board myself. And I helped Mama scour the old linoleum because, being the oldest, I had to kinda help raise the others."

Billy graduated from high school, was briefly in the Army, and spent an apprenticeship as a tool maker. Following the war, Billy, along with thousands of others, found himself without work. He got word of a possible opening with Connie B.

Gay, at that time a Disc Jockey with WARL radio in Arlington, Virginia, who was promoting Grand Ole Opry acts in that three-state area. He hitchhiked to Arlington, auditioned, and got the job.

In 1958, shortly after "Gotta Travel On" crested as a million-seller, Billy was signed as a regular cast member on the Grand Ole Opry. Billy was an instant hit, due in part to his professional experience with Jimmy Dean, Grandpa Jones, and Hawkshaw Hawkins during his pre-Opry days.

A superb instrumentalist, Billy was always in great demand as a session picker and soon turned his talents to the development of what was called "one of the finest flat-top guitars on the market"—the Grammer guitar. The first instrument came off the production line in 1965, and that premier guitar was donated to the Grand Ole Opry Museum.

Billy and his wife, Ruth, who were married in 1944, live in Illinois. Billy was inducted into the Illinois Country Music Hall of Fame in 1990, along with Tex Williams, Lula Belle & Scotty and Patsy Montana.

41

Becoming a member of the Grand Ole Opry on Dec. 23, 1967, was the icing on the cake for Jack Greene who had enjoyed one of the most successful years ever experienced by a country music artist.

That year his hit "There Goes My Everything" held the No. 1 position on the national charts for seven weeks, dropped to No. 2 for two weeks and then hit No. 1 again for another two weeks. His album by the same name stayed at the top of the charts for a year.

That year Jack Greene also dominated the Country Music Association Awards, winning Single of the Year, Album of the Year, Song of the Year and Male Vocalist of the Year honors.

The Maryville, Tenn., native had gone from being a drummer and singer for Ernest Tubb's Texas Troubadours to the top of the country music field in record time. And it was just the beginning.

He followed his 1967 successes with eight other No. 1 hits including "All The Time," "What Locks The Door," "You Are My Treasure," "Until My Dreams Come True," "Back In The Arms Of Love," "Love Takes Care Of Me," "Lord, Is That Me?" and "Statue Of A Fool." Greene also had two No. 1 albums, a hit single with Jeannie Seely and many award nominations, including several for Grammy Awards.

He's still earning honors. In 1989, Greene was inducted into the Atlanta Country Music Hall of Fame.

In recent years his performances have taken a charitable turn for a number of causes. In 1988 Greene participated in five benefit concerts in one month alone. More recently he was one of several Opry artists doing a benefit concert for R.O.P.E., the Reunion of Professional Entertainers, to raise funds for a retirement home for country musicians.

In 1990 Greene completed his first music video of his signature song, "There Goes My Everything," which aired on TNN: The Nashville Network's "Country Standard Time" series.

Also last year he and Ricky Van Shelton surprised and thrilled fans at the Superstar Spectacular show during Fan Fair with a duet performance on "Statue Of A Fool," a hit for Greene in 1969 and a hit for Shelton 21 years later.

A happy couple, June and Jack Greene.

"The awards are nice and I like to get them, but they are not the reason I sing. Music is my life and it is more important to me to please my audiences," Jack says seriously. "Nothing can take the place of those special feelings when you have played your best and the audience realizes this and shows their approval. I perform my music for me and for the people. If I can continue doing this, I am happy."

Tom T. Hall's songs captivate an attentive audience during a concert at Opryland USA.

Tom T. Hall is one of America's great balladeers, capturing in song the time-old story of the human condition. "I write songs so I can depict the inside workings of people," he says. "You try to establish a true voice—not colored by prejudice, politics or preference. If you're telling a story you have to separate all that, and just tell the tale. You must be honest. That's the main thing in songwriting." And his songs always have that focused, insightful quality, blending realism with sentimentality.

In a professional career spanning almost 30 years, Tom T. has written a variety of songs on such topics as sneaky snakes and old dogs to beer and miracles. Appropriately nicknamed "The Story teller," he writes and sings about subjects and people he has experienced in his life. As is the case with any truly gifted writer, Tom T.'s work contains all the elements of universal truth. It is his ability to convey the essence of life that attracts throngs of people to his concerts no matter where he performs.

Following an eight-year stint with the United States Army where he was stationed in Germany, Tom T. began his career as a disc jockey in Roanoke, Virginia. By this time the urge to write began to manifest itself and he started forwarding songs to publisher Jimmy Key in Nashville. Impressed with Tom T.'s songs, Key urged him to move to Music City. Tom T.'s salary as a writer was $50 per week, and he lived on this sum until his songwriting royalties started flowing in.

A member of the Songwriters Hall of Fame, Tom T. has earned one or more BMI awards each year since Jimmy C. Newman recorded "DJ For A Day," the first Tom T. Hall song ever recorded.

Tom T.'s solo recording career began in 1968 when he signed with Mercury Records. Since then he has had eleven number one records and has eight albums to his credit, including two very successful lps for children.

Some of Tom T.'s best known tunes include: "Ballad of Forty Dollars," "I Love," "The Year Clayton Delaney Died," "Old Dogs, Children and Watermelon Wine," "Sneaky Snake," "I Like Beer," "Your Old Man Loves You Honey," and "Country Is," among many others.

In addition, in 1968 Tom T. and Jeannie C. Riley became a famous team when the Hall-penned classic, "Harper Valley PTA" swept the national country charts. It sold over six million records and was the basis for a movie of the same name. So respected as a writer Tom T., at one time, had six songs in the charts recorded by other artists.

Tom T. has also authored three books, "The Laughing Man of Woodmont Coves," "How I Write Songs, Why You Can," and "The Storyteller's Nashville," which is not only an autobiography of his own life, but also chronicles the growth of the Nashville music industry. Tom T. rejoined the Grand Ole Opry in March 1980.

Despite fame and the increasing demands of his career, Tom T. is still a very private person. He leads a quiet life with his wife Dixie on their 60-acre farm, "Fox Hollow," south of Nashville.

GEORGE HAMILTON IV

George Hamilton IV, "The International Ambassador of Country Music," started out as a pop success, but quickly became one of the most enduring international country artists of all time. In 1956, George recorded the million selling record, "A Rose and A Baby Ruth," followed by teenage laments like "High School Romance," and "Why Don't They Understand," which hit the top 10 charts in the United States and Britain's top 20.

After his move to Nashville in 1959, George made his presence felt with a succession of country hits that included: "If You Don't Know I Ain't Gonna Tell You," "Before This Day Ends," "Fort Worth, Dallas Or Houston," "Truck Driving Man" and—his biggest country smash of them all—"Abilene." Moreover, he realized one of his life's ambitions and was invited to join the select cast of the Grand Ole Opry in 1960.

Record sales and chart success was only one side of the George Hamilton IV story. Soon, George began to look at markets and audiences outside of the United States. At first, through the material of writers like Gordon Lightfoot and Buffy Sainte-Marie, Canada loomed on the horizon, and then he began to explore the situations outside of the North American continent.

Since the mid 1960's George has worked hard at achieving international success, and very often his prime ventures into new territories were financed out of his own pocket. But the rewards have been immensely worthwhile. Today, his status as an international performer is beyond any dispute.

George IV is certainly the "first" when it comes to the international markets. George appeared at the first "International Festival of Country Music" at Wembley in 1969. He was the first American Country singer to appear in Russia and Czechoslovakia, and the first American to record an album in Eastern Europe in 1974. He was the first American Country singer to have his own British TV series, and has now done nine series for BBC-TV, including three in Belfast, Northern Ireland. He performed at the first "International Festivals of Country Music" in Sweden (1976), Finland (1977), Holland and Norway (1978), Germany (1979), Paris and Zurich (1980) and Vienna (1984). George appeared in England's First Country Music Summer Season Show, and

George signs autographs for fans during the annual Grand Ole Opry Fan Club festivities.

has now completed ten nationwide concert tours of Great Britain.

It was, however, this vast amount of international work that caused George to depart from Nashville and the Grand Ole Opry in 1971, and return to his native North Carolina homelands. He wanted to spend more time with his family— his wife, Tinky, and their two sons and daughter—as well as being readily available for television work in both North Carolina, Canada, and Great Britain.

In spite of his international popularity, George still wants to keep firm links with the American market. In 1976, he re-joined the Opry, and moved his family back to the Nashville area in 1986.

During recent months, this "International Ambassador" has maintained his role with activities around the world. Commencing with concerts in Japan, "Thanksgiving in the Country," in the United Kingdom, and concert tours of British churches. Following concert and television appearances in Prague with friend Jiri Brabec, he returned to Britain for his annual "Country Christmas" appearances. He also toured Europe as the narrator of "The Patsy Cline Story."

And today, more often than not, when you see George IV perform at the Opry or on tour the handsome fellow singing beside him is George Hamilton V, a chip off the old entertainment block.

The Opry audience is treated to a thrilling duet by Emmylou and her good friend, Vince Gill.

"The Indians have a saying," says singer Emmylou Harris from her Tennessee home. "The best way to catch a horse is to build a fence around it. I like to build fences around feelings and capture them with music." An apt metaphor, but it's hard to picture Emmylou Harris putting up fences. For nearly two decades, she has been one of music's premier bridge-builders, providing a vital link between folk, country and rock.

"Over the years I've done many different types of songs," she notes, "but in every case, they were songs I really responded to, that I really wanted to sing."

Born in Birmingham, Alabama, Emmylou Harris grew up near Washington D.C. As a college student in the late 60's, she sang with a local folk duo, eventually moving to Greenwich Village to make a stab at a professional music career. She played the clubs on the local folk scene, occasionally sharing the stage with legends like Jerry Jeff Walker and David Bromberg.

Emmylou began to draw attention on the club circuit in both New York and D.C. and in time was introduced to Gram Parsons, formerly of the Flying Burrito Brothers and a heralded pioneer in the burgeoning country-rock movement. Emmylou toured and recorded with Parsons until his tragic death in 1973. "After he was gone, I wanted to carry on with what I thought he would have wanted me to do," recalls Emmylou, "bringing certain elements of folk music, with its emphasis on the lyric, trying electric things, but always

coming back to that electric country base."

On her 1975 major label debut album "Pieces of the Sky", Emmylou introduced her Hot Band, which over the years has included such world-class players as Albert Lee, Rodney Crowell and Hank DeVito. Over subsequent years, she released a string of best-selling albums, including "Elite Hotel" (1976), "Luxury Liner" (1977), "Quarter Moon In A Ten-Cent Town" (1978), "Blue Kentucky Girl" (1979), "Roses In The Snow" (1980), "Evangeline" (1981, and "Cimmaron" (1982). Other recent albums include "Bluebird", "Angel Band", and "Cowgirl's Prayer".

As Emmylou moved closer to the heart of country music, she enjoyed seven #1 and 27 Top 10 hits including "If I Could Only Win Your Love," "Together Again," "Sweet Dreams," "Making Believe," "To Daddy," "Heartbreak Hill," and "Heaven Only Knows." In all, she has eight gold albums . Her 1987 "Trio" album with Linda Ronstadt and Dolly Parton is a platinum-plus success. And in 1992, Emmylou earned the highest honor a country artist can aspire to when she was inducted into the Grand Ole Opry.

With her enormous legacy of great music, Emmylou Harris today has no time for looking back. "I never listen to my old records," she says . "I'm always involved in the next thing I'm going to do. Hopefully, I've learned more as I've gone along, but I feel I have the same basic focus I've always had."

Jan shares a laugh with Grandpa Jones on the "Hee Haw" set.

Jan Howard is a very aware lady. Her credits speak for themselves. Professionally she's achieved the heights. In her personal life she's plunged to the depths. Yet she's risen above obstacles to emerge a stronger person, more compassionate human being, and a singer capable of moving an audience to tears with her ballads or bring laughter with her wit and charm.

In business where people come and go rapidly. Where overnight sensations are born and die just as quickly, Jan Howard has carved a solid niche for herself.

Jan was one of those lucky people to get a recording contract the first time a record producer heard her sing. She became an integral part of a syndicated television show almost from the beginning of her professional career. And there is a unique quality in her voice that sets her apart from all others. Jan has that warmth, strength, and compassion which comes from experiencing a life filled with highs and lows.

Back in West Plains, an expressway is named in her honor. That gives you some small indication of the esteem in which she is held at home. That love and respect, however, goes well beyond the area which has spawned so many country music greats. She is not only held in close regard by her thousands of fans, but also by those professionals within the music community.

Jan started in Los Angeles; she developed friendships with acquaintances who were beginning to write songs, and because of her obviously cooperative attitude, she was asked to sing one of the demonstration records of a song co-written by Buck Owens, intended for Kitty Wells.

Joe Johnson, a record producer on the West Coast, heard one of the demos, took the song, and this started Jan's recording career. She moved to Nashville in 1960.

Jan signed with Decca Records (now MCA) in 1965 and began cutting records with Owen Bradley. One hit followed another. On her own she cut many singles including "Evil on Your Mind," "Bad Seed," "Rock Me Back to Little Rock," and "Spinning Wheel." She also recorded some #1 duets with Bill Anderson including "Dissatisfied," "If It's All the Same to You," and "For Loving You." She was a part of the Bill Anderson Television Show for many years, and joined the Grand Ole Opry in 1971.

Jan has had more than her share of personal tragedy. Having lost two of her sons, Jimmy, the eldest, in Vietnam, and David, the youngest, four years later, Jan has softened the edges of tragedy with her love of God and the belief that He has a reason for everything and will give her strength to cope.

She has done many TV public service spots for the Armed Forces, Mental Health, and the Veterans Administration. Her efforts on behalf of the Vietnam Veterans and the Vietnam Veterans Memorial are legendary. And she devotes countless hours to other charitable endeavors. Her literary prowess was established with the publication of her autobiography, *Sunshine and Shadow,* a best seller by any standards.

This shy Missouri girl has traveled a long way from those humble roots to a prominent place in the annals of Country Music. Jan is a dynamite woman who is a survivor. "You can't change the past, and tomorrow is a dream," she advises. "The important moment in your life is today!"

Before his first album was released, when his success in music amounted to a small publishing company draw and endless one-nighters, Alan Jackson took a good, hard look at the industry he was entering. Country music, long dominated by an old guard, was being broken wide open, and the charts, airwaves, clubs and concert halls had been transformed into a free-for-all of new talent. That's great for the fans, of course, but a newcomer—even one as talented as Alan—could have been forgiven for being a little awed by the competition.

It's a measure of the man that it didn't turn out that way. Instead, with the mixture of determination and humility he'd been raised with, he referred to the highly appropriate George Jones hit, "Who's Gonna Fill Their Shoes," and said something that would be printed on his debut album: "I don't know whether I can fill 'em, but I'd sure like to try 'em on."

There's still some sorting to be done, but Alan Jackson has walked his first mile in those shoes, and it's been a very good mile indeed. There have been enough awards, nominations, chart-toppers, glowing press notices, and sold-out shows to fill anybody's scrapbook, and for the mechanic's son from Newnan, Georgia, the future couldn't look brighter.

In a very short period of time Alan released five consecutive number one hits: ("Here In The Real World," "Wanted," "Chasin' That Neon Rainbow," "I'd Love You All Over Again," and "Don't Rock The Jukebox"); sold more than 1.2 million copies of his debut album "Here In The Real World"; seen his second album, "Don't Rock The Jukebox," shoot to the top of the charts; and collected the Academy of Country Music's Top New Male Artist and Music City News Songwriters Awards' Song of the Year prizes along with two TNN/Music City News Awards. His third album: "A Lot About Livin' (And A Little 'Bout Love,) went double platinum and produced top singles: "She's Got The Rhythm (And I Got The Blues)," "Chattahooche," and "Mercury Blues."

Alan's appeal for the fans and media has involved much more than the music itself, though. He drives female fans to distraction with his blond-haired, blue-eyed good looks, while still managing to look like the lean, lanky guy from down the road who tempered his social life

One happy Alan Jackson fan gets an autograph and a photo during the annual Fan Fair festivities in Nashville.

with a lot of work on cars and a little music now and then.

Which is pretty much the way it was. While he was dating his high school sweetheart, Denise, he was also passionate about cars, buying, fixing and selling hundreds. Music grew slowly as an interest. He was 20 before he went to his first concert, and it was only after driving a fork lift and building houses that he decided to try and make a living from the music he'd performed in the area. He was 25, he had married Denise (they had a daughter, Mattie Denise, in 1990), and he decided to sell everything and move to Nashville. He took a job in the mailroom of the Nashville Network, made contacts, worked hard at writing, and went on the road with his own band.

While stardom has taken Alan by storm, his music is a sincere expression of "the real world" in which he was reared. His song "Working Class Hero" was written for his father upon his retirement from the Ford motor assembly plant, and "Home" is a tribute to Alan's Newnan roots.

On June 7, 1991, Alan got another home— the Grand Ole Opry. And the two are a perfect match. His music has been greatly influenced by some of the Opry's most famous members, in particular George Jones.

"There have been times when traditional Country Music has not been very popular," Alan says. "But the Opry kept it alive. If not for the Opry, some of the younger traditional Country Music singers would not have learned the style or been inspired to sing it."

STONEWALL JACKSON

Stonewall Jackson socializes backstage at the Opry with friends Bobby Osborne, left, and Melvin Sloan.

Stonewall Jackson is one of the recognized super stars of Country Music. He did it the hard way by recording an almost unbroken string of hit records over an astounding period of 17 years. So no one in the music industry was surprised when his first single on the MGM label, "Herman Schwartz," turned out to be another blockbuster. For 16 years he was one of the brightest stars on the Columbia label. More than 20 of his records ranked number one in the popularity charts and more than 50 of them were in the top ten. His 23 albums were best sellers.

In short, Stonewall Jackson was a hit-maker! and "Herman Schwartz" was just the next hit to follow the hit "House of Bottles and Cans." Over the years "Waterloo" and "Don't Be Angry" are two songs that have become indelibly linked with Stonewall Jackson. Everywhere he goes audiences scream for these songs. He always sings them both. They have been good to him. "Waterloo" was a million-plus seller. And since 1956 Stonewall has been one of the brightest stars of the world-famous Grand Ole Opry.

Born in Tabor City, North Carolina, he was the youngest of three children. His father died when he was only two. Already poor, the family faced a grim future. Mrs. Lulu Jackson decided to move to South Georgia to her brother-in-law's farm where the opportunities for work seemed better. All this happened during the depression years. Lacking money for travel, the family hitch hiked to Georgia. "I was plowing at the age of eight and pulling a crosscut saw in the woods by nine," Stonewall recalls, "but with God's help we survived."

"By the time I got out of the Navy in 1954, I wanted to make music my career," Stonewall said. But first he had to save some money. So he went back to South Georgia to work on the farm—and to save. And then everything good happened to Stonewall Jackson all at once. He traveled to Nashville in his new pick-up truck and visited Acuff-Rose Publishing Company in an effort to sell some songs. Wesley Rose listened, liked the songs, and more important, liked the singer. He called his friend, "The Solemn Old Judge," George Hay at the Grand Ole Opry and sent Stonewall down to WSM Radio to Judge Hay. Judge Hay listened to a couple of songs, and Stonewall was signed to an Opry contract. "Ernest Tubb, Roy Acuff and the management of the Opry lent me a hand when I needed one the most. I had no record, I was poor, I had no amount of money, no record contract and I didn't even have a decent guitar," Stonewall recalled. "I borrowed one for quite some time from other acts on the show."

Lots of fans ask if Stonewall is a nickname or Jackson's real name, and he proudly tells them it is his real name. He is descended from the famous Confederate General, Thomas J. Jackson, whose bravery in the face of enemy fire earned him the immortal nickname Stonewall.

In 1991, Stonewall finished his biography: *From The Bottom Up.* It's the Stonewall Jackson story as told in his own words.

There's a refreshing farm atmosphere to the Brentwood, Tennessee home of Stonewall Jackson and his family. Their comfortable home perches on a hill overlooking a nine-acre lake which Stonewall calls Lake Waterloo. It is a great spot for fishing and song writing, two of Stonewall's favorite activities.

Jim and Jesse's Opryland Bluegrass Festival help celebrate Opryland's 20th season of entertaining America.

For brothers Jim & Jesse McReynolds Grand Ole Opry membership is a family affair—literally.

The sons of talented musicians, Jim and Jesse grew up singing together on the family farm in their native Coeburn, Va. Both learned to play stringed instruments and as teenagers honed their unmistakable harmony by singing traditional mountain music at local gatherings.

Jim, who sings a clear, polished tenor and plays guitar, is two years older than Jesse, whose distinctive style of mandolin playing has come to be known as "McReynolds" or "cross-picking." Complementing these instruments is the five string banjo and the fiddle, always features of their band, the Virginia Boys.

Jim & Jesse made their radio debut on a Virginia station in 1947 and remained there until 1952 when they moved to a station in Lexington, Ky. That same year they signed their first recording contract with Capitol Records.

As their reputation grew with bluegrass fans, Jim & Jesse became regulars on radio and television shows throughout the South and soon earned national acclaim.

Songs such as "Are You Missing Me," "Border Ride," "Sweet Little Miss Blue Eyes," "I Wish You Knew," "Drifting and Dreaming of You," "Ole Slew Foot," "Cotton Mill Man," "Better Times A' Coming," "Diesel On My Tail" and "Paradise" are just a few of the top songs that established Jim & Jesse as one of the top duos in the world.

As the popularity of bluegrass grew in this country, so did the reputation of Jim & Jesse, and they were invited to join the Grand Ole Opry in 1964.

In recent years they have been honored with a star in the Country Music Hall of Fame "Walkway of Stars," membership in Bill Monroe's Bluegrass Hall of Fame, induction in the Virginia Country Music Hall of Fame and numerous awards for their many musical accomplishments.

In addition to Capitol Records, they have recorded more than 30 albums on Epic Records, Opryland Records and, in recent years, on their own label, Old Dominion Records. In 1990 they released a 26th anniversary album on Rounder Records.

They are frequent guests on popular television programs and at bluegrass festivals throughout the nation, and the world.

Jim & Jesse have made several appearances at the Wembley Festival in London as well as in Switzerland, France, Holland, Ireland, Austria, Sweden and Germany. They also recorded a two-record album titled *Jim & Jesse—Live in Japan* during a Far East tour. More recently they enjoyed a highly successful tour in Africa for the State Department.

When they aren't touring, Jim & Jesse can be found back "home" at the Grand Ole Opry, entertaining fans with their unique style of bluegrass that has earned them international acclaim.

Two Country Music legends, George Jones and Bill Monroe, acknowledge the enthusiastic response from an appreciative audience.

Few performers in any field of entertainment find a life time of commercial success and the respect and adolation of their peers. Some reach the heights of stardom but few truly become the superstar. George Jones has attained those ultimates as an entertainer. His collective successes, his unique stylism and his consistent ability to relate emotion to his fans have made him a true living-legend in Country Music.

In 1956, his single, "Why, Baby, Why" reached the national top ten charts and virtually every record since has ascended to the same heights. In the last twenty years, George Jones has recorded over 500 songs on over 100 albums, and sold millions of records. Literally no one, including George, knows exactly how many records have been released. He rejoined the Opry in 1973 after a short absence.

The man nicknamed "the Possum" has scores of hit country songs which read like signposts of the genre's history. A few include: "There Ain't No Money In This Deal;" "Why Baby Why;" "Window Up Above;" "She Thinks I Still Care;" "The Grand Tour;" "White Lightning;" "Bartender's Blues;" "The Race Is On;" "I Always Get Lucky With You;" "He Stopped Loving Her Today;" and "Who's Gonna Fill Their Shoes."

The professional music career all started for George as a teenager in the late 1940's, when radio station KTXJ in Jasper, Texas gave him an afternoon show. From there it was on to bigger things—sharing a half hour program with Eddie and Pearl in Beaumont for room and board and $17.50 a week, and working a little in his free time in local clubs. In November 1950, he enlisted in the Marines, beginning the only interruption in a career that has shown consistent growth.

Born in the southeast Texas town of Saratoga, not far from Beaumont, George had been introduced to music early. His church pianist mother and his truck-driver/pipefitter father who played guitar, got him a guitar of his own and he soon was picking, singing, writing and performing with a group of his own.

George was working as a house painter and just getting back into the club circuit in 1953 in Texas when he was discovered by the founders of a new record label in Beaumont. The discovery was looked on as the reincarnation of the spirit the world thought it had lost when Hank Williams died at the beginning of the same year.

Of course it really hasn't been that easy for George who's trials and tribulations are the stuff of legends and food for countless newspaper and magazine pieces. Today George says, "I never went into this business even thinking about money, what I would do or where I would go. I just wanted my guitar in my hand and to keep going. I just wanted to sing."

And sing he has.

GRANDPA JONES

Two old country boys, Grandpa Jones and Bashful Brother Oswald (Pete Kirby), along with Oswald's bride, Eunita, share a joke in the backstage area.

When Grandpa Jones joined the Grand Ole Opry in March 1947, he was only 33 years old, but he had already been a "grandpa" for 11 years.

Louis Marshall Jones was born in Niagra, Ky., in 1913, the youngest of 10 children. His share-cropper father moved his family from farm to farm. Grandpa recalls at age 10 sneaking in and "foolin'" with a guitar left in their house for safe-keeping by a farm worker. Later one of his brothers came home with a guitar for him. It only cost 75 cents, but that's what Grandpa used when he began playing local dances and parties with a friend.

In 1928 the family moved to Akron, Ohio. Two years later Marshall Jones got his first break in the music business, winning first place over 450 contestants in a week-long amateur contest. The next day he got a radio job on WJW in Akron and used his $50 prize money to buy a better guitar.

While there he teamed up with the harmonica player Joe Troyan. The two later moved to a Cleveland radio station which led to a stint in the house band for the popular "Lum and Abner" radio show. When that show moved to Chicago, Jones and Troyan, billed as Zeke and Harve, moved to WBZ in Boston. There they joined Bradley Kincaid's troupe.

It was on that early morning radio show that Kincaid would say, "Come on an' get up here to the microphone; you're just like an old grandpa." That, coupled with the way Grandpa talked (which made him sound older), caused fans to write in asking how old is that old man, and Grandpa Jones was born.

He was only 22 years old at the time, but a pair of 50-year-old boots, a false bushy mustache, fake white eyebrows and wrinkles drawn on his face enhanced Grandpa's image.

He worked at several radio stations in West Virginia before moving to one in Cincinnati. World War II found him serving as an MP in the Army in Germany. While there, he organized a band called the Munich Mountaineers which played daily on the Armed Forces Radio Network.

After the war in 1946, Grandpa Jones moved to Nashville and worked with Pee Wee King on a tent show. This led to appearances on the Grand Ole Opry, and he was made a member in March 1947.

His guitar was traded for a banjo which he plays using the drop-thumb technique. This distinctive banjo pickin' style and his down-home country humor made him a natural for the television show "Hee Haw" when it made its debut in 1969.

The man who has been associated with such songs as "Old Rattler," "Good Ole Mountain Dew," "Eight More Miles to Louisville" and his version of the Lonzo and Oscar hit "I'm My Own Grandpa" was inducted into the Country Music Hall of Fame in 1978.

During his long career, he has recorded numerous albums on a variety of labels and toured extensively. His wife, Ramona, who plays fiddle and other instruments, often joins him on tour.

His book, *Everybody's Grandpa, Fifty Years Behind the Mike*, was published in 1984. In 1988 fellow Opry and "Hee Haw" cast members and other music industry greats honored Grandpa Jones for his 60 years of contributions to country music.

He still performs regularly on the Opry and during Opryland's season Grandpa and other favorite cast members perform "Hee Haw Live" in the Roy Acuff Theater.

He looks very much like he did in 1935—only now the mustache and eyebrows are his own. And he still wears the same pair of boots Bradley Kincaid gave him almost 60 years ago to help transform Louis Marshall Jones into "everybody's favorite grandpa."

HAL KETCHUM

Hal thrills the Opry audience with another eloquent performance.

Whoever called Country Music "White Man's Blues" must have been talking about Hal Ketchum. His work has the soulful edge of an R & B performance with the lyric insight and strength you might find if William Faulkner had lived in Music City U.S.A. and penned some country songs. He's one of the most accomplished song stylists and interpretive singers in any music genre, and as a writer, Hal's talent pool appears to be amazingly deep and rich in material.

This former carpenter from upstate New York moved to Texas in 1981 and, inspired by local tunesmiths, began writing his own songs. Hal bought a house in Gruene, unaware that he was just across the river from one of the oldest, hippest music halls in Texas. "The day I moved in, I was exhausted and resting, and I heard this Western swing music creeping in through the window." Hal got up to investigate and discovered that Asleep at the Wheel was playing less than two football fields away.

A drummer since high school in his hometown of Greenwich, New York, Hal also had a notebook full of song ideas, but he didn't give much thought to becoming a songwriter until he started regularly attending Gruene Hall's Sunday afternoon singer/songwriter sessions. "I was around all these great writers, people I really respected, but I was inspired more than intimidated," he recalled. "Everybody was real supportive. It wasn't like some contest."

In 1989, Hal recorded his first album, "Threadbare Alibis," for the tiny Austin label, Watermelon Records. A little later he decided to move to Nashville and try to make a living as a songwriter. The problem was that his demos were too good, and Dick Whitehouse of Curb Records quickly offered Hal a recording contract.

The result of "Past The Point Of Rescue," his gold debut Curb album, has been nothing short of phenomenal. The first single, "Small Town Saturday Night," became 1991's biggest song of the year in *Radio & Records*. He followed that release with three more hits: "I Know Where Love Lives," "Past The Point Of Rescue," and "Five O'Clock World." *Music Row* Magazine named his video for "Small Town Saturday Night" the breakthrough video of the year (all three of his videos have hit #1). Hal's album, "Sure Love," showcases his considerable songwriting skills. Included are: "Daddy's Oldsmoblile," "Hearts Are Gonna Roll," "Softer Than A Whisper," "Mama Knows The Highway," and "Trail of Tears."

Hal joined the Grand Ole Opry on January 22, 1994. "Until I started playing the Opry I didn't realize how powerful it is," he said. "The first time I played it I felt a real power—the power of heritage, of tradition, of the written word."

The day he became an Opry member, Hal expressed his personal feelings with the following poem:

A long time ago, in my very childhood,
Marty Robbins told me of trouble in El Paso.
I was in the kitchen, I remember it was
*   wintertime.*
Summer was for play, Winter for reflection.
More time underfoot, more time to listen.
The snow piled up, the little house hummed
*   and shook.*
Ray Charles was busted.
Buck and the Buckeroos had a tiger by
*   the tail.*
Patsy Cline descended like an angel on a
*   staircase of strings.*

I loaded sixteen tons with Ernie Ford
And studied the written word with Roger Miller.
My Father brought these people home, one by
*   one, and they all stayed.*
They told me even then that I was welcome,
They knew I understood.
A thousand songs and singers
Have beckoned me to his hallowed place,
And tho'some would say I've come a long way,
I would say simply,
That tonight, I arrive.

Peace, Hal

On July 3, 1993, Alison Krauss became a member of the Grand Ole Opry at twenty-one, when most people are just starting their careers. And Alison was the first bluegrass artist in nineteen years to be inducted into the Opry.

When Alison Krauss first appeared as a guest on the Grand Ole Opry, she was seventeen years old. Alison remembers, "We couldn't believe we were there, standing on the same stage and playing and singing through the same microphones as all those great artists we'd heard on the radio even before we started playing music.

"It is such an honor to become a part of what has been a monument in the history of country music. We are all so privileged to be accepted by the great aritsts and musicians who make up the Grand Ole Opry," Alison noted. "Bluegrass has always been a part of country music, and with all the changes in country music today, it's wonderful to see that the Grand Ole Opry still has strong beliefs and pride in bringing bluegrass bands to its family. And we're so happy that Bill Monroe, Jim and Jesse, and the Osborne Brothers think we're okay!"

Alison Krauss is an inspiration to a whole new generation of budding blue grass musicians, setting new standards and breaking new ground with her records, performances and accomplishments. While her music is rooted in traditional bluegrass and she remains deeply committed to the form, her willingness to draw from other influences has made her music accessible not only to fans of bluegrass, but to those of other styles of quality music.

One of Alison's finest talents is her ability to find and arrange great songs. Whether she's drawing from a bluegrass standard, a regional songwriter or a pop record, she uses her instincts to come up with the perfect complement of voices and instruments for the song. Her skills as a musician and singer are equaled only by her sense of restraint and good taste.

Alison grew up in Champaign, Illinois, where her parents encouraged her and her brother, Viktor, to take up instruments at an early age. Soon after, she began playing the violin. Alison discovered fiddle contests and bluegrass festivals and became a convert to the musical form she loves the most. Though her initial acclaim was as an instrumentalist, a standout young fiddler who

Garth Brooks inducts a surprised Alison Krauss into the Opry family.

won championships, Alison's voice soon became what everyone was talking about.

At age 14 she recorded her first album on Rounder Records, "Too Late To Cry," and by age 18 had earned a Grammy nomination for her 1989 Rounder release "Two Highways." The following year Alison won the Grammy for Best Bluegrass Recording for "I've Got That Old Feeling." This album generated singles and videos of the title song and "Steel Rails" and was named International Bluegrass Music Association's (IBMA). The IBMA also named her Female Vocalist of the Year for 1990 and 1991, and 1991's Entertainer of the Year.

Alison and her band, Union Station, captured a second Grammy in 1992 for "Every Time You Say Goodbye." The album, picked by the *New York Times* and *USA Today* as one of 1992's ten best albums, has yielded the singles "New Fool," "Heartstrings" and "Every Time You Say Goodbye."

Dolly Parton, one of Alison's biggest fans said, "I can't think of a person more suitable for country music and the Grand Ole Opry than Alison Krauss. She has one of the sweetest, most honest voices that I have heard since the early days of what we call traditional country music.

She is a country girl, pure of voice, pure of heart …and I truly wish her well in this business."

Hank checks his mailbox at the "Opry Post Office" backstage.

There's leprechauns . . . Londonderry . . . limerick . . . and then there's Locklin. Hank Locklin is the lilt of Country Music. With a voice that sounds like "a little bit of Heaven," Hank has been the Number One country singer in Ireand for many years.

"I've never kissed the Blarney Stone," he'll quickly admit; but Hank doesn't need that added luck of the Irish, for he's the Lucky Irishman.

Hank Locklin is lucky, Irish and has made such a name for himself in Ireland, England and Germany that Pee Wee King calls him "Europe's Amassador of Country Music."

If Hank Locklin wears titles well, it's pride that makes him that way. Born Lawrence Hankins Locklin in McLellan, Florida, into a family that usually reared doctors, Hank wanted to be an entertainer instead. By the time he was ten, Hank was picking guitar for amateur contests in Milton, Florida, and, as a teenager, he was already a featured performer on radio station WCOA in Pensacola. He enjoyed athletics in school but much preferred singing and playing guitar for school parties and plays. Until he was able to perform professionally, Hank worked at various jobs in his home state: farmer, ribbon mill hanker, and shipyard worker.

His big professional break came in 1942, when he made his concert debut at the Community House in Whistler, Alabama. There followed a series of tours, broadcasts and personal appearances through the deep South. Hank became an RCA recording artist in the mid- 1950s and quickly was elevated to star status in Country Music.

The luck was with Locklin, and he was asked to join the Grand Ole Opry in 1960.

The success of Hank Locklin has become legend since then. In addition to his numerous awards for "Send Me The Pillow That You Dream On," Hank has an ASCAP Award for the LP "Country Hall of Fame" and "Where The Blue Of The Night Meets The Gold Of The Day" plus Cash Box and Juke Box awards for "Please Help Me I'm Falling" and a NARAS Award for "Locklin Sings Hank Williams."

And Hank Locklin's success continues. It seems the luck and signs are with Locklin . . . but, mostly, the tremor-tenor voice is with him, and that's why Hank is loved by so many fans around the world.

Charlie Louvin visits with his little buddy Shotgun Red at a TNN studio.

Combining talent, hard work, and an almost unlimited devotion to his art has earned Charlie Louvin his Country Music Legend status.

"Country Music is the only life I know," says Charlie with a proud grin. "I guess that's why I put so much more into my music and stage work."

What Charlie Louvin puts in a song is the "I've been there" kind of emotion that makes listeners and audiences agree with him, whether the score is a broken home, a love gone bad, or the bottom of a bottle. If it's Country, Charlie's been there . . . from the Sand Mountain region of Alabama to the foxholes in Korea. He plowed some hard rows in his life, but he always manages to break the way for his continued success. The success that he calls: "Pleasing my fans and friends and family . . . they're everything to me."

Charlie and Ira Louvin, two farm boys from Alabama, first tasted the fruits of applause when they toppled the competition in a talent contest in Chattanooga. But it was touch and go for quite awhile, and they thought they would have to give up Country Music. Somehow, he and Ira made it through and became members of the Grand Ole Opry in 1955, just three years after they had signed with Capitol Records. After Ira's untimely death in 1965, Charlie stayed with the Opry and

Capitol, becoming one of the grandest little guys in Country Music. Whatever tears were to be shed were put into the words of such great top ten songs as: "Will You Visit Me On Sunday," "See The Big Man Cry," "Mama's Angels," "I Don't Love You Anymore," "Funny Man," "When You Fly Alone," "Love Don't Care" with Emmylou Harris, and numerous duets with Melba Montgomery, with whom he shares a Grammy Award.

Charlie's latest album is: "Charlie Louvin 50 Years of Makin' Music" on Playback Records. This album features Charlie makin' music with friends: Willie Nelson, Waylon Jennings, George Jones, Charlie Daniels, Crystal Gayle, Tanya Tucker and Melba Montgomery.

It is not unusual that this country boy and his late brother, Ira, made their great mark in the country field with religious songs. Charlie's walls are decorated with plaques and awards and gold records for such beloved songs as "Weapon of Prayer" and "Family Who Prays." In 1979, Charlie accepted for the Louvin Brothers as they were inducted into the Songwriters Hall of Fame. The Brothers wrote over 500 songs. Charlie is a consistent performer making approximately 200 appearances a year.

PATTY LOVELESS

Porter Wagoner proudly introduces Patty Loveless to the Opry audience.

Patty Loveless, whose name was added to the Grand Ole Opry roster in 1988 next to her distant cousin, Loretta Lynn, was practically destined for Opry membership. The Pikeville, Ky., native remembers sitting on the kitchen table at age three or four listening to the Grand Ole Opry on Friday nights while her mother mopped the floors. By age five she sang along.

At age 12 she began singing with her brother, Roger, and two years later with him made her first visit to Nashville. The trip led to a meeting with Porter Wagoner. After hearing the then 14-year-old girl sing during that first meeting, Porter told her someday she would be a star.

Soon after, Opry stars The Wilburn Brothers hired Loveless to replace their departing "girl singer" Loretta Lynn and signed her as a staff songwriter. The next few years she spent her winters in Louisville, Ky., finishing high school and her summers in Nashville pursuing her music career.

Marriage and a move to North Carolina interrupted the pursuit of her dream, but Patty returned to Nashville in the mid-1980s. She garnered critical attention after the release of her first MCA album, *Patty Loveless,* in 1986. That LP contained the singles "Wicked Ways" and "I Did" and two Top 40 country hits, "After All" and "Lonely Days, Lonely Nights."

Opry membership came on June 11, 1988, shortly after her second album, *If My Heart Had Windows,* was released. Its title song became Patty's first Top 10 hit. The LP also yielded the hit "A Little Bit In Love."

Patty's third MCA album, *Honky Tonk Angel,* produced three Top 10 hits, "Blue Side of Town," "Don't Toss Us Away" and "Lonely Side of Love,"

as well as the singer's first two No. 1 hits: "Timber (I'm Falling in Love)," which stayed at the top of *Radio & Records'* charts for three consecutive weeks in 1989 (a feat no female singer had accomplished since Dolly Parton's "9 to 5" in 1981), and the 1990 hit "Chains."

Her fourth album, *On Down the Line,* was released in 1990 and has produced three Top 10 hits, "On Down the Line," "The Night's Too Long" and "I'm That Kind of Girl."

In addition to recording her own hit singles, Patty is in demand as a duet artist. She added the harmonies to labelmate Vince Gill's 1990 CMA Song of the Year and Grammy Award-winning "When I Call Your Name" as well as his single "Pocket Full of Gold."

This new generation Opry star has collected her own share of awards. She won the 1989 American Music Award for Favorite New Artist Country and in 1990 was named Female Artist of the Year in the fan-voted TNN Music City News Awards. Recently the 1991 *R&R* Country Radio Readers' Poll named her Best Female Artist.

Patty, who can sing traditional country equally as well as honky-tonk, blues, rockabilly and, yes, even "rock-tinged" music, says "I like to always put at least one song on each album that is different from the rest. It wakes people up, surprises them. And I really think people like that."

Fans certainly like it when this young artist—who used to stand backstage at the Ryman Auditorium, watching all the stars perform and dreaming of being a part of this tradition—goes on the Opry stage to sing her "music with a little edge" for the audience in the Opry House and for young radio listeners in kitchens throughout the land.

Another Opry magic moment! For the first time, Loretta and sisters, Peggy Sue and Crystal Gayle sing together on the Opry stage.

If a performer's importance is measured by the ability to rise above categories, then Loretta Lynn again confirmed her artistic importance when she stepped onstage in Los Angeles to accept the 1985 American Music Awards' Award of Merit in recognition for her exemplary career. The award wasn't for country or pop or any other such limiting designation—but rather for the power and inspiration of Lynn's own distinctive music. Trends come and go, while Loretta Lynn continues as a national treasure.

When "Ladies Home Journal" named Loretta among its 100 most important women in America, the honor was understandable. For beyond her reputation as a performer and songwriter, she has developed into that rarest of social creatures: a woman who can be admired by career women and homemakers alike. She's experienced the best and worst of both roles.

"The only time I ever hurt myself," she recalls, "was when I was working so hard and worrying about it—worrying about being away from my kids while they were growing up. But finally I just got to thinking that there's nothing I can do about it. They're going to grow up no matter what I do."

If Loretta spoke to one group of women with her controversial tribute to "The Pill," she spoke just as eloquently to another with her lovingly harried tribute to motherhood called "One's On The Way."

In the course of her performing, Loretta has sung for three presidents, been the subject of a Barbara Walters and a "20/20" special, acted on "Dukes of Hazard" and "Fantasy Island" and is a sought after guest on "The Tonight Show," "Good Morning America," "The Today Show," and "CBS Morning News." She was the first woman to win the Country Music Association's Entertainer of the Year award and went on to win the Academy of Country Music's Artist of the Decade award. She is a member of the Nashville Songwriters Association's Hall of Fame, and the Country Music Hall of Fame. She joined the Grand Ole Opry in 1962.

All in all, it's been a rather diverse trail for the little Kentucky-born housewife who started off in 1960 with a long-shot called "I'm A Honky Tonk Girl."

Loretta is branching out in her writing. She is assembling material for a follow-up book to "Coal Miner's Daughter." Instead of beginning where the best-seller left off, the new book, Loretta promises, will start with her earliest memories—as a two-year old. There was drama aplenty in her life even then, she asserts: "I didn't walk until I was four years old, and I was given up to die three times." This book, she predicts, will also become a movie.

As hard as it's been, life never disappoints her. "How in the world can you have a fiction story that's half as good as the truth?"

Mel McDaniel's search for success in Country Music has proven to be a long and arduous journey, one that has seen him steadily build upon an increasingly solid foundation throughout the years toward a long-lasting career as a singer, performer, and songwriter. Nominated for prestigious Country Music Association's "Horizon Award" and inducted into the Country Music Hall Of Fame's Walkway of Stars" on the strength of the super successful LP "Let It Roll" and what has become known as "the blue jeans record," Mel has become a new, although very mobile, country landmark. Two additional CMA nominations for "Baby's Got Her Blue Jeans On" as "Single of the Year" and "Song of the Year" confirm his new vantage point. Even more recently, he has been breaking attendance records consistently at performances across the country, taping his second career video "Stand Up" for release in conjunction with the new album, and making appearances on such television programs as Nashville Now, Bobby Bare and Friends, New Country, and Hee Haw.

Music videos and television are playing an increasingly important role in a career that, interestingly enough, first began under the inspiration of Elvis Presley on TV. At age fourteen the Oklahoma native taught himself the chords to "Frankie And Johnny" and has literally been performing ever since.

After graduation from high school, he married and set out to make a living for his family. Despite a brief move to Nashville, he soon found himself playing to packed houses in Anchorage, Alaska, a move that allowed him to stretch and grow as an entertainer as he developed his own singing style. A couple of years went by and Mel returned to Nashville once again, landing a job as a demo singer and soon signing as a songwriter with Combine Music through the efforts of renowned music publisher Bob Beckham. In 1976, Capitol Records signed him to a contract and his debut single, "Have A Dream On Me," was an instant success, paving the way for the hits that lay ahead.

What followed was a string of Top Ten country classics such as "Louisiana Saturday Night," "Right In The Palm Of Your Hand," "I Call It Love," "Big Ole Brew," "Ole Man River (I've Come To Talk Again)," the beautiful McDaniel-

Mel delivers a foot-stomping, hand-clapping performance on the Opry stage.

penned ballad "God Made Love," and of course the hit singles "Let It Roll," and "Baby's Got Her Blue Jeans On." He joined the Grand Ole Opry in 1986. The success of Mel's songwriting escalated as well. Hoyt Axton was the first ever to record one of his songs with "Roll Your Own." Then Conway Twitty recorded "Grandest Lady Of Them All." Mel also wrote, along with Dennis Linde, a song entitled "Good-bye Marie" that Kenny Rogers included in his multi-million selling Kenny LP. Johnny Rodriguez and popster Bobby Goldsboro each followed with his own hit version of the song.

With his recent chart successes, three CMA award nominations, the release of his LP's, continued songwriting, and the high demand for personal appearances, many might think that his long search is complete. Yet for Mel McDaniel, the journey has only begun. Fortunately, Mel's "Worn Out Shoe" is also a very comfortable shoe . . . one that he can "Stand Up" in for a long time to come.

We can divide the history of Country Music into periods represented by its most influential artists. Depending on our years, Country Music can mean Patsy Montana, Molly O'Day, Kitty Wells, Patsy Cline, Loretta Lynn, or Tammy Wynette. For the 1980's and beyond, Country Music means Reba McEntire.

The daughter of a schoolteacher and an Oklahoma rancher who didn't make it beyond elementary school, Reba, the third of four children, grew up taking risks. Her father and grandfather were world-champion steer ropers, a talent she inherited and one that served her well when she traveled the rodeo quarter-horse barrel-racing circuit. At the National Finals Rodeo in Oklahoma City in 1975, Reba sang the national anthem and was discovered by a Nashville songwriter. Within a year, she had a recording contract.

Since that time, she has won just about every award bestowed upon an entertainer. Reba has been honored by: the Country Music Association; Academy of Country Music; TNN/Music City News; Rolling Stone; American Music Awards; NARM; and been awarded a Grammy. Reba joined the Grand Ole Opry in 1985.

"I tend to center my songs for women," she says. "I know a song is right when I hear it, just like I know a dress is right when I put it on. The wonderful thing is that even though I look for songs that speak to women, I find that when women like them, the men like them too."

Among her chart topping hits are: "(You Lift Me) Up To Heaven," "I Can't Even Get The Blues," "You're The First Time I've Thought About Leaving," "Whoever's In New England," and "Fallin' Out of Love." Four of her albums have been certified Gold, signifying sales in excess of a half million records each.

"At a time when people have to ask what Country is, she's a singer of the Country song," says her friend, Emmylou Harris. "I just like to be called a good singer or a bad singer," Reba says. "I don't mind them comparing me to Patsy Cline or Loretta Lynn because then they're talking about me."

Change comes naturally to Reba. "I change my stage show twice a year," she says. "If I don't have songs and a show that are creative and keep me interested, I'm in trouble. My Momma said

Country Music fans vote a happy Reba McEntire another "TNN Music City News Country Award."

that when I was born, my attention span was zilch, and it's gone down hill from there."

In addition to her God-given pipes—at once equally comfortable turning out ladylike boogie, Western swing, and the kind of soulful ballads that can shatter a truck-driver's heart—Reba loves to entertain.

And what part of all this does Reba like best? Recording? Producing? Performing? Roping steers? She doesn't even hesitate.

"The whole thing," she says with a twang that can bend guitar strings and break hearts. "I like all of it."

The press has called her "a bundle of talent," "a glamorous, sexy star," and "a totally together lady." She calls herself "a hopeless ham and an occasional show-off." But no matter what descriptions are popping up, there's one that will always fit Barbara Mandrell . . . she is a winner!

A show business veteran of over 25 years, Barbara continues to come out on top. Her list of awards keeps growing. She is the first artist to ever win the Country Music Association's coveted "Entertainer Of The Year" award two years; the CMA twice voted her "Female Vocalist Of The Year;" she has received eight People's Choice awards; nine awards from the fan-voted Music City News, including the Living Legend Award; the Tex Ritter Award from the International Fan Club Organization; a Grammy; a Dove Award; and induction into the National Association for Sport and Physical Education Sports Hall of Fame.

Barbara was born December 25, in Houston. Her mother, Mary, began teaching Barbara the accordian before she could read. Her father, Irby, sang and played guitar. Her family moved to Oceanside, Ca., while Barbara was still a youngster, where her father bought a music store. By the time Barbara had reached her teens she had learned to play steel guitar, saxophone, banjo, and bass guitar. She made her television debut, at age 11, on a live local show called "Town Hall Party," and appeared, at age 13, on ABC's "Five Star Jubilee." Her father eventually formed a family musical group, "The Mandrells," with Barbara, her mother and father and two young men on guitar and drums.

In 1967, she married that drummer, Ken Dudney, temporarily gave up her musical aspirations, and became a serviceman's wife. Their family now consists of children, Matthew, Jaime, and Nathaniel. Ken was overseas in the Navy when she moved with her family to Nashville. During a subsequent visit to the Grand Ole Opry she felt the tug of the footlights once again. Halfway through the show Barbara turned to her father and said, "Daddy, if you'll manage me, I'd like to try to get on the other side of the microphone again, I wasn't cut out to be in the audience." She joined the Grand Ole Opry in 1972.

Some of her hit records include: "Midnight Oil," "Standing Room Only," "Sleeping Single in a Double Bed," "Married, But Not to Each Other,"

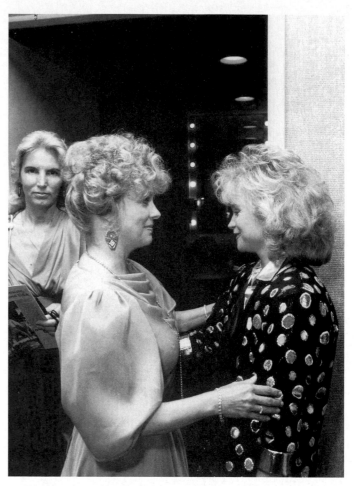

Two dynamite blonde country singers, Connie Smith and Barbara Mandrell, share a private moment backstage at the Opry.

"Years," and "If Loving You Is Wrong."

On the evening of September 11, 1984, Barbara had a major brush with death in a head-on crash near her Hendersonville, Tennessee home. Only minutes before the crash, for some fateful reason, Barbara had suggested that Matt, Jamie and she should buckle-up. Until that moment, she had never been a seat-belt user. Since then she has completed national Public Service Announcements available on audio, video and poster, strongly urging the public to "Please buckle up, you may never get another chance."

Blonde, blue-eyed, and standing five feet tall, Barbara Mandrell reflects her strong faith and drive in her positive outlook on life. "If there's a decision to be made," she says, "I simply put it in God's hands . . . and things just begin to fall into place."

Blind since birth, entertainer Ronnie Milsap has never felt limited in any area of activity that he has ever undertaken. Says the handsome six-footer "I believe the Good Lord blesses each of us with some special ability or talent, and I've always tried to make the best of what I have instead of bemoaning over things I don't have." This is proven true by the facts, that at the age of seven, young Milsap was a violin virtuoso; at eight, he played the piano; by twelve, he had mastered the guitar. Now he plays all keyboard instruments, stringed instruments, percussion instruments and all woodwinds.

Ronnie was born in Robbinsville, North Carolina, a small farming community near the Tennessee-North Carolina border. At the age of six, Ronnie was sent to the State School for the Blind in Raleigh. It was at this excellent school that Ronnie's aptitude for music was discovered and developed.

After completing high school in Raleigh, Ronnie attended Young-Harris Junior College near Atlanta, Georgia. After finishing the junior college, he stayed on in Atlanta picking up a job here and there as a sideman. Then Ronnie formed a band and went to work steadily playing clubs and colleges. In 1969, Ronnie and his group moved to Memphis, Tenn., and started work at T. J.'s, a popular Memphis club.

In 1973, Ronnie, his wife Joyce and their son Todd decided that they should move to Nashville, Tenn., the country music capital. Before you could say "Music City, U.S.A., Ronnie was signed with RCA Records and had released a two-side hit, "All Together Now (Let's Fall Apart)" and "I Hate You." "That Girl Who Waits On Tables" was next, the "Pure Love" and the Country Music Association 1974 Male Vocalist of the Year award. Then "Please Don't Tell Me How The Story Ends," a Grammy winner.

The hits just keep on coming: "A Legend In My Time" (with the album of the same name capturing the 1975 CMA award as Album of the Year), "Too Late To Worry, Too Blue To Cry," "Daydreams About Night Things," "(I'm A) Stand By My Woman Man," and "It Was Almost Like A Song" (with the album of the same name winning the 1977 CMA award for Album of the Year).

Ronnie and friend, Lorianne Crook, relax at Ronnie's home just before the TV cameras roll.

Other top selling RCA albums include: "Greatest Hits," "There's No Gettin' Over Me," "Greatest Hits Volume 2," and "Lost In The Fifties Tonight." "True Believer" is his top-selling album for Liberty Records.

1976 was a magic year for Ronnie because he won both the CMA award for Male Vocalist of the Year and the NARAS Grammy award for Best Country Vocal By A Male Artist (for "Stand By My Woman Man"). Ronnie iced the cake in 1977 by once again winning the awards for Best Album of the Year, he also won in 1978, and Male Vocalist of the Year and by winning the most coveted of all country music awards, Entertainer of the Year. He has since won three more Grammy awards, numerous Country Music Association awards, and RCA has credited Ronnie with six Gold Albums, one Double Platinum Album, and the only Gold Braille Album ever to be awarded.

Bill Monroe proudly accepts a special handmade mandolin from Opry President Hal Durham during Bill's 50th Anniversary celebration.

It's only natural that Bill Monroe would work for WSM Radio. Those are the initials of William Smith Monroe, the man who brought his own unique style of music to the Grand Ole Opry over 50 years ago.

The Rosine, Ky., native was only 28 years old when he joined the Opry cast on Oct. 28, 1939. Introduced by George D. Hay, the Opry's founder, Bill performed "Muleskinner Blues" and got three encores that first night at the War Memorial Auditorium.

Bill describes his beloved bluegrass as a music with "a hard drive to it. It's Scotch bagpipes and ole-time fiddlin'. It's Methodist and Holiness and Baptist. It's blues and jazz and it has a high lonesome sound. It's plain music that tells a good story. It's played from my heart to your heart, and it will touch you. Bluegrass is music that matters."

Bill's bluegrass evolved from the folk and Country Music he heard growing up in Kentucky in a musical family. Orphaned by age 11, he was raised by his uncle, Pendleton Vandiver, an excellent country fiddler and mandolinist. By age 12, Bill was backing up his Uncle Pen at local dances.

In the 1920s he and brothers Birch and Charlie formed a band and played together until the late 1930s. In 1938 Bill formed his first Blue Grass Boys band, a group that has spawned the careers of such artists as Lester Flatt, Earl Scruggs, Mac Wiseman, Stringbean, Sonny Osborne and Vassar Clements.

In the 1940s, Bill began adding lyrics to his melodies and wrote such classic hits as "Blue Moon of Kentucky" and "Uncle Pen" which today remain his most requested numbers.

He recorded with Victor and then Columbia Records before signing with Decca (later to merge with MCA). Through dozens of albums and more than 50 million records sold, Bill has remained with MCA. His 1988 *Southern Flavor* LP for MCA won the first Grammy Award ever given for bluegrass music in 1989. In conjunction with his 50th Opry anniversary, MCA released *Bill Monroe and the Blue Grass Boys Live at the Opry*, which received a Grammy nomination.

Honors are many. The Father of Bluegrass was inducted into the Country Music Hall of Fame in 1970. In 1986 a U.S. Senate resolution recognized "his many contributions to American culture and music." A direct descendant of President James Monroe, he has performed shows for Presidents Jimmy Carter and Ronald Reagan.

When he isn't playing the White House or the Opry, Bill and his Blue Grass Boys are doing between 150 and 200 dates a year. This Opry veteran has sponsored the annual Bean Blossom Bluegrass Festival in Indiana for over 25 years.

When Bill made his Opry debut, Judge Hay told him, "If you ever leave the Opry, it'll be because you fired yourself." Bill has no plans to "fire himself."

In the 50th anniversary LP's liner notes, Opry President Hal Durham noted how Bill created a music style, maintained it through difficult times, expanded it internationally and touched people's lives everywhere he went, or wherever his music was heard, and added, "That is why we at the Opry feel so fortunate to have had this gentleman as a member for 50 years."

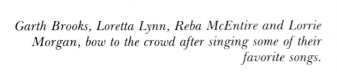

Garth Brooks, Loretta Lynn, Reba McEntire and Lorrie Morgan, bow to the crowd after singing some of their favorite songs.

"You can't imagine how it felt the night I became a member of the Opry in June of 1984. The first time I could really call this place my home, I couldn't stop shaking, or trembling, or crying," Lorrie recalled.

"Emotionally, music is one of the most overwhelming professions in the world. Every time you turn a crowd on with a song, they let you know. We honestly work as much for the applause, the cheers, and the whistles, as we do for the money," she says, "It's definitely an emotional thing—music."

If Lorrie's emotional about her music, she's also realistic. She knows what it takes to please. Her elegant vocal style has been featured on Ralph Emery's popular "Nashville Now" television show on The Nashville Network. In 1984, Lorrie appeared on CBS' Academy of Country Music Awards as a final nominee for the New Female Vocalist of the Year. No doubt you've seen her pretty face on many of your favorite country TV programs.

When she's not on the road entertaining, or in front of the lights of a TV camera she's most likely to be found at home with her guitar. A talented writer, as well as a musician, she spends much of her spare time in the studio laying down tracks for her songs or taping demo sessions for other artists.

Lorrie has recorded for Hickory Records, MCA, and RCA Records. All of her releases have been fan favorites from her first single, "Train Wreck of Emotion," through "Dear Me," and "A Picture Of Me (Without You)." Lorrie has many chart hits earning her nationwide popularity.

Listen closely to Lorrie and, as she admits, you'll hear a blend of the country music she grew up with. Her main influence, of course, was her father, the late George Morgan, who's legendary smooth vocals thrilled country fans from 1948 until his early death in 1975. A member of the Grand Ole Opry for 26 years, George was most remembered for his smash hit "Candy Kisses" in 1949.

But in 1959 he left behind another legacy. Because on June 27, he and wife Anna became the proud parents of their fifth and final child—a pretty little green-eyed girl they would call Lorrie. Now, just barely 5'5" with her heels on, the little green-eyed girl has become a full fledged lady. A veteran stage performer, and a favorite among country fans throughout America, Lorrie is likely to make a lot more friends before she's through. A native Nashvillian, the mother of a beautiful daughter and handsome son, one of four girls in a family of five children, she's a noted swimming enthusiast who loves "the ocean, softball games, and picnics," and like her father in 1949, Lorrie Morgan was 24 years old when inducted into the Grand Ole Opry. History has a way of repeating itself.

JIMMY C. NEWMAN

Grand Ole Opry audiences are treated to a variety of styles of music, ranging from traditional and contemporary country to folk, gospel, bluegrass, rockabilly and Cajun.

Cajun music, which has been around for some 200 years, originated in Nova Scotia by the French people living there. Exiled by the British in the 1700s, they settled in Louisiana and developed their own culinary and music culture.

Now, two centuries later, the Opry's chief proponent of Cajun music is Jimmy C. Newman, a native of Big Mamou, La., who was raised in the traditional Cajun style. This Opry veteran and his band Cajun Country combine the centuries-old sounds of Southern Louisiana's bayous with modern country music. Mixing the traditional Cajun accordian and fiddle with bass, drums. electric lead and rhythm guitars and Jimmy C's bilingual vocals, they generate a oneof-a-kind style.

Ironically, this form of music wasn't what brought Jimmy C. Newman to the Opry in August 1956. As a teenager, he played and sang country songs of all kinds, particularly cowboy songs of his hero Gene Autry. Later, he sang with a band in Big Mamou and played clubs and theaters in the South and Southwest before getting the chance to host his own radio show in Lake Charles, La. That led to membership on the radio and TV show the "Louisiana Hayride" in Shreveport and resulted in a recording contract with Dot Records in the early 1950s.

In 1954 he enjoyed his first hit, a song he cowrote titled "Cry, Cry Darling." Several Top 10 hits followed, along with Opry membership. In 1957 his No. 1 country hit "A Fallen Star" was a crossover hit on the pop charts.

While he continued to enjoy success with traditional country hits, he also added songs such as the 1961 hit "Alligator Man" and 1962's "Bayou Talk" and the 1963 album *Folk Songs of the Bayou* which renewed his ties with his Cajun roots.

In 1978, he formed his band Cajun Country and began performing such classics as "Jole Blon," "Jambalaya," "Colinda," "Diggy Diggy Lo" and "The Cajun Stripper."

Since 1980 he and his band have traveled to Europe annually, touring in England, Spain, Germany, Holland, Ireland, Sweden and France to enthusiastic crowds. They still tour Europe at least once a year.

With a big Cajun yell, Aaaiiieeee! Jimmy C. gets the Opry House energized.

Jimmy C. teamed with other Southern Louisiana music stars Doug Kershaw, Eddy Raven, Queen Ida and Rockin' Sidney for the first-of-its-kind Cajun Fest '91. This series of concerts throughout the U.S. featured Cajun music along with real Cajun food. The tour generated a TNN special titled "Cajun Country."

Some of Jimmy C. and Cajun Country's latest achievements are a 1991 Grammy nomination for their Rounder Album, "Alligator Man," and a special award in 1992 from the Cajun French Music Association of South Louisiana recognizing Jimmy's contribution to promoting Cajun Music worldwide. In 1993, Jimmy and his band appeared in the CBS TV movie "Conviction," playing and singing traditional Cajun Music.

Jimmy C. and his wife, Mae, continue to make their home on their 670 acre "Singing Hills Ranch," in Rutherford County, Tennessee, not far from Music City and the Grand Ole Opry. And Opry fans know it's time to *laissez les bon temps rouller*—let the good times roll—when "the Alligator Man" opens his set with his signature, high pitched Cajun yell, Aaaiiieeee!

THE OSBORNE BROTHERS

Sonny and Bobby entertain thousands at Fan Fair's annual Bluegrass Concert.

Born in the mountainous coal mining region of Southeastern Kentucky in the little village of Hyden, it came natural for Bobby and Sonny in later years to sing "Nine Pound Hammer," "The Knoxville Girl" and other great coal mining songs and Folk ballads of the Appalachian Mountains.

Because of a six year age difference the brothers did not start out as a team but rather began their careers separately and at different times. Both, however, made their way on pure raw talent, playing and singing the traditional songs, some of which they had learned as boys in Kentucky. Through a succession of towns and radio stations they gained individual recognition. The brothers got together as a team in 1953, following Bobby's discharge from the U.S. Marine Corps.

Their recording debut on a major label came in 1956 with MGM Records. These recordings today rank among the all time classic examples of Osborne Brothers style, featuring Bobby's distinctive and unequaled natural high lead voice and joined by Sonny's rich baritone. It was on these recordings that they changed the customary arrangement of trio harmony parts to create a new and completely unique sound in voices, thus giving their records a larger and fuller sound. The MGM releases of the late fifties clearly marked The Osborne Brothers as a Country Music group of importance.

In 1963 they signed with Decca Records (now MCA) and during August, 1964 became regular members of WSM's Grand Ole Opry in Nashville. The Decca recording established the successful practice of featuring the Osborne "big voice" sound, while giving greatly increased prominence to the instrumental wizardry of the two Osbornes, Sonny with his five-string banjo and Bobby with his mandolin. Sonny's intricate backup note patterns and clear, strong lead work on the banjo, often in a radically different "single string" fashion are featured heavily. At the same time he has accomplished the difficult feat of also bringing out the pulsating and insistent "drive" for which the instrument is justly famous. Bobby's individualistic mandolin stylings have been described as "bluegrass jazz" and to the utter delight of audiences he often lays his mandolin down and demonstrates the fact that he is also an expert "hoedown" fiddler.

The Osborne's hit records include: "Making Plans," "Up This Hill And Down," "Midnight Flyer," "Take Me Home, Country Roads," "Muddy Bottom," "Tennessee Houndog," "Georgia Pineywoods," "Kentucky," "Ruby," and "Rocky Top."

A magic moment at the Grand Old Opry! Porter and Dolly harmonize together again.

To the world-at-large, Dolly Parton, with her outrageous fashions, her golden gossamer wigs, her sparkling jewelry and her lively wit, has always created a larger-than-life image wherever and whenever she has performed. Her music, concerts, starring film roles, Dollywood entertainment complex in the Great Smokey Mountain region and cosmetic line have all contributed to making Dolly an internationally-known figure of gigantic proportions.

Dolly Parton left the East Tennessee hills at the age of 18 with a cardboard suitcase full of songs. She had been honing her craft since the age of seven and was determined to build her future on it. Dolly set out bringing songs to Nashville producers and record labels, sometimes singing them accompanying herself on guitar, sometimes presenting demos if she could afford them. Music City was, in her eyes, the city of hope and promise and she set a pace of success that would eventually lift her to the top of her profession.

Dolly's songs have captivated listeners by making them feel and understand slices of life. Emmylou Harris had this to say about the Parton penned song "To Daddy" that she released as a single. "To me it's like an O'Henry short story. Dolly sets you up and then whammo…she turns it all around. When I first heard it my lips were trembling and I was afraid I was gonna make a scene."

Dolly herself has proven the ability to perform her music in a way that forms legions of fans, from the evolution of her first album to her, "Here You Come Again," for which she earned her first Gold. Dolly was first discovered by the country market with her natural country heritage, but then other music markets became aware of her outstanding compositions and delivery. Universal appeal became highly evident and Dolly Parton was becoming a household name.

The first professional singing Dolly did at age 10 was for The Cas Walker Radio Show. Prior to that she tuned up in church along with her sisters (her family boasted 12 children). By her early teens she had cut her first record and soon after arriving in Nashville Dolly signed with RCA Records and became a member of Porter Wagoner's syndicated television show. Dolly joined the Grand Ole Opry in 1969.

Dolly has been honored with every important award. She has three Grammys, numerous Country Music Association Awards, an Oscar nomination, Golden Globe nominations, gold and platinum singles and albums, and many honors from the music industry magazines. But, in between her many projects and honors, Dolly always returns to songwriting, touring and live performing. "Nothing beats getting out on stage and singing direct to my fans, the people who've been my friends all through the years, as well as some of the new friends I've made along the way," says Dolly.

Even though she's accomplished so much with her career, to Dolly it's just the beginning. "Everybody wants to be successful at whatever their inner dream is," she says. "I'm not near finished with what I want to do, with what I want to accomplish yet. I want to be somebody that left something good for somebody else to enjoy."

A glorious occasion, Minnie's 50th Opry Anniversary! From left: Carol Lee Cooper, Jimmy Dickens holds the sculpture of a WSM Grand Ole Opry microphone adorned with her trademark hat presented by Opryland's Chairman of the Board Edward L. Gaylord, husband Henry Cannon, Connie Smith, Hank Snow, Roy Acuff, and Grant Turner.

When a very nervous 28-year-old comedienne told her first joke on the WSM Grand Ole Opry on Nov. 7, 1940, she didn't know whether she would be invited to return for future performances. She was. And, over 50 years later, she is still entertaining fans with tales of Brother and all the folks from Grinder's Switch, Tennessee.

Minnie Pearl was paid $10 for her performance on the Opry in the War Memorial Building and, never having been before a microphone, remembers being scared to death. Grand Ole Opry founder George D. Hay, the Solemn Old Judge, recognizing her fright, gave her some advice she would remember and share with others through the years.

"Just love 'em, honey, and they'll love you right back," Judge Hay told the young comic just before she went on the air that first Saturday night. She did, and the fans did. She received more than 250 pieces of mail from her first performance. A week later Minnie Pearl was invited to become a regular Opry cast member.

At the time she joined the Opry family, Minnie Pearl was just four years old, according to Sarah Ophelia Colley Cannon. She had patterned the young country girl after a sprightly mountain woman from Baileyton, Ala., she had met while producing an amateur musical comedy there in 1936.

After staying in this woman's mountain cabin for 10 days and listening to her tales and funny stories, she began imitating the woman and people laughed. Heeding her father's advice to "Keep her kind, daughter. Keep her kind," she created her character and, combining two familiar country names, called her Minnie Pearl.

Minnie's first professional performance in costume was in 1939 before the Pilots Club in Aitken, S.C. She bought her whole costume at a salvage store there.

When she began performing on the Opry the following year, Minnie Pearl did so in a hat without the now familiar price tag. She probably started wearing the price tag in 1942 and she decided on the $1.98 price because she thinks that's what the hat cost in 1939.

Minnie Pearl also has collected many stories over the years and many of these were recorded on albums in the 1940s and 1950s. "She has withstood the rigors of time because probably she's no threat to anybody. She's not pretty. She's not sexy. She's not smart, and people just sort of think they're safe with her. Wives know that the husbands are not going to flirt with her," explained the woman whose friends call her Minnie. That's what she prefers. "I've been Minnie longer than I've been Sarah," she explained.

As Minnie, clad in a gingham dress and white stockings, she has entertained throughout the world, worked tirelessly for charitable causes and won numerous awards. Her efforts for the American Cancer Society, coupled with a personal bout with breast cancer in 1985, led to her being named the 1987 recipient of the Society's National Courage Award. That same year she won the Roy Acuff Humanitarian Award for Community Service. Among her many other honors was her selection as the first comedienne inducted into the Country Music Hall of Fame in 1975. In 1988 she was the first recipient of a newly created Minnie Pearl Award, now presented annually by The Nashville Network.

Stu Phillips and Jim Ed Brown wait patiently in their duck blind, trying to keep warm, at the annual Grand Ole Opry Duck Hunt.

When his name was added to the official roster of Grand Ole Opry stars in 1967, Canadian-born Stu Phillips achieved a lifelong ambition. His earliest memories of music are of tuning a crystal set in Calgary to the sounds of the Opry in faraway Nashville, and what he heard set his career and his goal.

"I love the Opry," says Stu, "It's a tradition, a way of life for Country Music fans; an institution with substance and meaning for its followers. I want my career to have a similar meaning, and that means dedication and hard work."

Stu Phillips was born in Montreal in Canada's French speaking province of Quebec. He ventured west at an early age and settled in Calgary, Alberta in the foothills of the Canadian Rockies, an ideal environment for this creative young man, who wrote many of his early songs in this setting.

Other than a very brief interest in becoming a lawyer, Stu's one goal all his life has been show business. From performing at social parties in church to various radio shows: the "Noon Specials" and the big "Saturday Night Jamborees," of radio fame just a few years ago. He soon progressed to television and his recordings became favorites. He became an immediate success on

TV and has consistently had his own television show. He has appeared on most of the top syndicated television shows in America and on national TV with stars such as Johnny Cash, Tennessee Ernie Ford, Carol Lawrence, Leslie Uggums and Danny Thomas.

Stu has traveled extensively: to the Far East, the Middle East, Africa (where his records have received the equivalent of gold records), to Europe on three occasions, and the interstates and highways of the U.S. and Canada.

He is married to a beautiful Canadian girl, Aldona, and they have three grown children. A girl, Leagh, and boys, Joel and Jasson.

On the personal side, Stu is interested in people, particularly some of the upcoming talent. He truly believes the greatest investment a man can make is in people. "I would have nothing if it had not been for people investing in me—from a 50 cent picture bought by a fan, to much larger investments by those in a position to allocate funds for budgets for recording sessions, TV series and so on," he adds. "And I will always be grateful to those who placed their faith in me; I can only repay this debt by passing it on, that is, placing my confidence in others."

Once upon a time a young man had a dream to be a country music singer and a star of the world famous Grand Ole Opry. That young man was Ray Pillow and the dream began in 1963 when he loaded a U-Haul trailer with everything he owned and headed to Nashville with his wife, Joanne and their three children Dale, Selena & Daryl.

Within three years the reality of that dream began to unfold with the signing of a recording contract with Capitol Records, being voted "Most Promising Male Vocalist" in all trade magazines, and most importantly in 1966, becoming the 50th member of the Grand Ole Opry.

In addition to recording, touring around the world, and performing at the Grand Ole Opry, Ray was always interested in other facets of the business. As early as 1964 he and his good friend and manager, Joe Taylor, started what is now one of the oldest booking agencies in Nashville, The Joe Taylor Artist Agency. Later he was instrumental in bringing Lee Greenwood to Nashville, securing his recording contract with MCA Records, and signing him to his publishing company, "Sycamore Valley Music". Out of this venture, not only came the Country Music Association's 1985 Song of the Year, "God Bless the U.S.A.", but also became the campaign song for both President's Reagan and Bush.

An ironic turn of events occurred in January 1990 when his friend, Jimmy Bowen, President of Capitol Records, made him Director of A & R, at the label that had launched his career 25 years earlier.

Today Ray Pillow is a happy man! His dream has been fulfilled and even more, his story continues...

Above: Daughter Selena and sons Dale and Daryl Pillow.

Below left: Joanne and granddaughter Ali-Ray.

Below right: Ray's birthday party, July 4, 1993! With his grandchildren: Brody, Cory, Ali, and Zachary.

Charley Pride has had an illustrious music career. For the past quarter century, Charley has been one of the Top 20 bestselling artists of all time. His body of work includes a legacy of 36 #1 hit singles, over 25 million albums sold worldwide, 31 gold and 4 platinum albums—including one quadruple-platinum. And talk about longevity, "Pride! My 6 Latest & 6 Greatest," is Charley's 51st album; it reunites two of the greatest legends of country music, Charley Pride and his original producer, Jack Clement.

Born to poor sharecroppers as one of eleven children in Sledge, Mississippi, Charley unofficially started his music career as a ballplayer in the Negro American League with the Memphis Red Sox singing and playing guitar on the team bus between ballparks. Self taught on a guitar bought at age 14 from Sears Roebuck, Charley would join various bands on stage as he and the team roved the country.

After a tryout with the New York Mets, Charley decided to return to his home in Montana via Nashville. It was there he met manager Jack Johnson, who upon hearing the singer play, sent him back to Montana with the promise that a contract would follow.

One year later, Charley went back to Nashville where he was introduced to producer, Jack Clement, who gave him several songs to learn. On a subsequent trip to Music City, Clement upon hearing Charley's renditions of the tunes asked the fledgling singer if he could cut two songs in two hours. Pride agreed and "The Snakes Crawl at Night" and "The Atlantic Coastal Line" were recorded.

Three months later, Charley broke into the industry for real when Chet Atkins and RCA Records liked the two song demo enough to sign him. His first single hit the airwaves in January of 1966 and Charley's star was on the rise .

Charley's biggest public appearance in support of the singles was at a show held in Detroit, hosted by Ralph Emery. When Charley stepped on stage he was greeted with loud applause, which got lower and lower in volume until near silence as most of the audience began to make the realization that he was a Black country singer. But, Charley's music prevailed and after the show he was besieged with autograph seekers and the rest, as they say, is history.

Charley Pride waves to the Opry fans after his induction as a member of the Grand Ole Opry cast.

Between 1969, when he first hit the number one spot on the singles charts with "All I Have To Offer You (Is Me)," and 1984, when he commanded the number one spot with "Every Heart Should Have One," he had scored more than 36 number one singles.

Dozens of charttoppers Charley has scored in the past years now stand as modern classics. "Kiss An Angel Good Morning" went on to be a million-selling crossover single. Other memorable hits include "Is Anybody Going to San Antone?," "I'm So Afraid of Losing You Again," "Mississippi Cotton Picking Delta Town," "Someone Loves You Honey," "When Stop Leaving I'll Be Gone," "Burgers and Fries," "Mountain of Love," and "You're So Good When You're Bad," to name a few.

On May 1, 1993, 26 years after he first played there as a guest, Charley Pride joined the Grand Ole Opry. And just in case music should leave his blood, Charley continues to work out annually with baseball's Texas Rangers and when not touring extensively worldwide or recording music, Charley can often be found pursing another love, one at which he also excels, golf.

Charley met the love of his life, Rozene, while playing baseball in Memphis. They have been married for over 35 years and raised sons Kraig and Dion and daughter Angela. He and his family currently reside in Dallas.

Mike Snider's latest yarn gets a large chuckle from Jeanne.

The Total Entertainer Is...one who writes hit songs, one who performs beautifully on stage, one who can hold an audience in the palm of her hand the entire length of the show. That is the perfect description of Jeanne Pruett.

Small town crowds and sophisticated city crowds alike love this personable lady. She has one of the best road bands in the business. Not only does most of her band sing, but they do duets, trios, and even an occasional foot tappin' gospel quartet number or two. The Jeanne Pruett show is exactly that, it's a show. The lady takes Country Music to new heights. She's lovely. Whether you're attending a concert, fair, club, park, or rodeo, you can be assured you are getting one of the best shows in the business.

Jeanne Pruett is R.F.D. Country. Pell City, Alabama is her home town. She is one of 10 children born to a full-time farmer, part-time cotton mill father and mother who both had a great love for Country Music and a deep appreciation for Jeanne's talent. Jeanne and her husband, Eddie Fulton, have bought a one hundred sixty acre ranch and farm outside of Nashville.

The Grand Ole Opry is a long way from the farmlands of Alabama, but through hard work, honest effort, and great talent and years of writing hit songs for other greats; Marty Robbins, Conway Twitty and Tammy Wynette, the lady made it in 1973. The following year was none the less eventful. After three years of playing to packed houses all over Europe, Jeanne was named Female Vocalist of the Year in London, England. Jeanne was nominated by the Country Music Association the same year for Female Artist, Song of the Year, Record of the Year, and Album of the Year, all for her wonderful song "Satin Sheets." Billboard Magazine also honored her with awards for Female Album as well as Best Album of the year in 1974.

1985 was an exciting time for Jeanne. What better place than her annual Fish Fry and Show during Fan Fair to sign a record deal. With most of the membership of her fan club present, Jeanne signed with MCA/DOT Records. Most recently is Jeanne Pruett's Feedin' Friends Cookbooks.

Her work for Retarded Children of the World has never ceased. The Shrine Burn Hospital of America has honored her countless times for her efforts on their behalf. Jeanne tries to, as she says, "Put something back into the business for all the great things it's given to me."

Del Reeves, Wilma Lee Cooper and Bill Monroe are among the many artists who sign autographs and visit with the fans attending the annual Grand Ole Opry Birthday Celebration held in October.

He's a singer, impressionist, stand-up comedian, actor, songwriter, television and stage personality, and versatile musician with an abundance of never ending energy. Off stage, Del is one of the most amiable, easy going and dedicated persons in show business.

Del Reeves' recordings have been solid chart makers for over a decade and include seven number one records. His biggest hits were "Girl On The Billboard," "Philadelphia Phillies," "Take Me To Your Heart," "Swinging Doors," "Ain't Nobody Gonna Get My Body But You," and "Slow Hand."

A native of Sparta, North Carolina, he began singing and playing guitar as a small boy. By the time he was 12 years of age, he was playing with a band on a regular Saturday radio show. "I was the youngest of 11 children, and we all sang and played. I had four brothers in World War II, and when they left home, they left their old guitars laying around. I got to playing around with them, and little by little, learned to play. My Mother used to tune the guitar for me," he recalls.

Del attended Appalachia State College in Boone, NC, and served in the US Air Force for four years. While stationed at Travis AFB in California, he began his recording career with Capitol Records. Following his discharge, Del decided to remain in California, where he was developing a reputation in the music world as a singer-writer-performer.

Del was beckoned to Nashville by his friend and fellow songwriter Hank Cochran in 1962. In 1965, he struck gold with "Girl On The Billboard," followed by a string of some 25 hit singles in the years following.

On the strength of his superb showmanship and million selling record, in 1966, the multi-talented Del realized a lifelong dream when he was invited to become a regular member of the world famous Grand Ole Opry.

As his popularity grew, Del hosted his own television show "Del Reeves Country Carnival." Success in the music field also led to his appearing in eight movies. The last, "Sam Whiskey," starred Angie Dickenson, Clint Walker and Burt Reynolds.

Del, whose real name is Franklin Delano (after President Roosevelt) lives outside of Nashville and enjoys the quiet life of a rural community and the beautiful countryside.

The number of Del Reeves fans continues to grow, and his peers respect his talent.

Mel Tillis says "He's Fan-T-T-Tastic."

Roy Clark says "He's the greatest."

The "Cowboy Way" is the only way for Riders In The Sky. They have been busy reacquainting a very hungry audience with the one important ingredient too often forgotten in American music: the rich heritage of the West.

Fortunately the three "saddle pals" have committed their extraordinary talents to reclaiming that lost territory for a grateful public. Since the first of their eight Rounder LP's appeared in 1980, they have unabashedly brought forward a genre that was thought to have perished in the 1950s as surely as the "singing cowboy" movies themselves. Not content merely with flawless recreations of the work of such originators as the Sons of the Pioneers, the Riders have transcended the category of "novelty act" by deftly weaving original compositions into their albums without disrupting their distinctive flavor. Their latest album is: *Merry Christmas From Harmony Ranch* for Columbia Records.

What makes these times particularly gratifying for Riders In The Sky to expand their devoted following, though, is their proven ability to captivate live audiences. Moreover, the Riders' appeal extends to those people on whom the future health of the Country Music business clearly depends: children (for whom the group specially assembled an LP). The Riders have hosted their own weekly award-winning radio program, "Riders Radio Theatre" since 1988 on National Public Radio across America, have starred in their own weekly Saturday morning children's program on CBS-TV, were acclaimed in the film "Sweet Dreams," hosted The Nashville Network's "Tumbleweed Theater," and are subjects of a collection of skits and biographical information, "Riders In The Sky: The Book." They joined the Grand Ole Opry in 1982.

Ranger Doug

Ranger Doug, "The Idol of American Youth," is six feet and a hundred and a few too many pounds of rugged Western manhood. His eyes are green and what's left of his hair is brown. He is the groups' MC, plays rhythm guitar, sings baritone in the trio, yodels, and writes many of their original tunes.

Always smiling, always courageous, Ranger Doug is a true singing cowboy hero for the 1980s:

It's happy trails again when Riders In The Sky get to harmonize backstage with their favorite cowboy, Roy Rogers.

a straight shooter, a square dealer, and a real dull guy. "It's not the easy way," he says, "but it's the cowboy way!"

Woody Paul

Woody Paul is a long, lean, lanky six-footer. He has soulful blue eyes, a strong nose, stronger ears, and right kissable lips, especially if you like the flavor of partially used snuff. Woody sings tenor in the trio, and is known from border to border and cheek to cheek as the King of the Cowboy Fiddlers. He's the master of a number of instruments, including guitar, five string banjo, harmonica, and the electric campfire, and his rope twirling has earned him a national reputation as the King of the Clothesline.

Too Slim

Too Slim is a cheerful feller with a smile as big as Montana and a gleam in his blue eyes some folks mistake for intelligence. And yes, he really is too slim, though he's not as slim as Woody, which causes endless confusion.

Too (as his close friends call him) sings lead in the trio, and is a master of his "bunkhouse bass." He's the chief comedian of the outfit as well: Senor Too Slim, Side Meat, and Too Jaws are but a few of his alter egos.

His hobbies include salting slugs, riding drag, and creating music on various parts of his body.

Johnny introduces another bearded entertainer to the enthusiastic Opry fans.

When the Grand Ole Opry invited Johnny Russell to join its roster in August 1985, the radio show added a veteran entertainer who just happens to be a singer, songwriter and a comedian—in no particular order.

A Sunflower County, Miss., native, Johnny moved with his parents to California at age 11 and as a teenager grew up in an entertainment atmosphere. He began acting, appearing in clubs and on local TV and writing songs at a young age.

One of his first songs ever recorded has earned him many dollars even though few recognize the title. The song, entitled "In a Mansion Stands My Love," was the B side of Jim Reeves' "He'll Have To Go," the No. 1 country hit of 1959. Johnny frequently tells audiences how he has collected royalties from a million-seller for a song few remember.

He also laughs about the song he tried unsuccessfully to get recorded for two years before Buck Owens made it a hit in 1963 and the Beatles' Ringo Starr followed suit a few years later. The two re-recorded "Act Naturally" as a duet and produced a music video of the song in 1989.

Others who have recorded Johnny Russell songs include Burl Ives, Dolly Parton, Patti Page, Loretta Lynn, the Wilburn Brothers, Del Reeves and Gene Watson with "Got No Reason Now For Going Home."

While he has written hits for others, Johnny also has enjoyed success as a recording artist with such songs as "Mr. and Mrs. Untrue," "Rain Falling on Me," "Rednecks, White Socks and Blue Ribbon Beer," "The Baptism of Jesse Taylor," "Catfish John," "Hello I Love You," "Ain't No Way To Make a Bad Love Grow" and "Song of the South."

Johnny, who suffered a mild stroke in 1987, underwent triple bypass heart surgery in January 1989. However, he was back at work by April 29, performing at the annual Johnny Russell Day in his hometown of Moorhead, Miss. Proceeds from the annual event, started in 1988, are used for the Johnny Russell Scholarship Fund at Mississippi Delta Junior College.

He also raises money for the scholarship fund through sales of his *Johnny Russell's Country Cookin' Cookbook,* a collection of low cholesterol, low calorie recipes.

Johnny still tours and is the first country artist to perform live on British Satellite Broadcasting (BSB). This new cable and satellite TV network aired Russell's performance at the 1990 International Music Festival at Wembley Arena in London.

Whether he's appearing on satellite in England or on the Opry stage in Nashville, Johnny Russell entertains with a mixture of traditional country songs and down-home country humor.

Jeannie Seely and "Opry Backstage" producer Janet Tyson await their cue to begin the live Saturday evening show.

Four-year-old Jeannie Seely was barely tall enough to turn the knob and not really able to see the numbers on her family's big console radio. But when she found 650 (WSM) on the dial, that's where the indicator stayed, her mother recalls.

Jeannie, who was born in Titusville and raised in Townville, Penn., even remembers sitting in the family's Ford, eating popcorn and drinking soda pop and listening to the Grand Ole Opry on Saturday nights while her parents played cards at friends' houses.

By age 11, she was performing on a weekly show on a radio station in Meadville, Penn. Years of playing auditoriums, small clubs and country music parks; a two-year stint as a disc jockey on her own Armed Forces Network show; and executive secretarial positions with Liberty and Imperial Records in Hollywood followed before she moved to Nashville in 1965.

A recording contract with Monument Records led to her first hit record entitled "Don't Touch Me" in 1966. The single went to No. 1, won her the 1966 Grammy Award for the Best Female Vocal Performance, Country and led to Opry membership in 1967.

Other hits—including "Can I Sleep In Your Arms," "Lucky Ladies," "Little Things," "Tell Me Again," "I'll Love You More" and "Please Be My New Love"—enabled her to tour throughout the world and appear on several television shows and earned her the nickname of "Miss Country Soul."

For 11 years she toured and sang with fellow Opry member Jack Greene. The popular duet team performed everywhere from New York's Madison Square Garden to London's International Country Music Festival. The two also enjoyed consistent Top 10 duet hits, including the No. 1 "Wish I Didn't Have To Miss You," "What In The World Has Gone Wrong With Our Love," "Much Oblige" and "You And Me Against The World."

When she wasn't writing hit songs for herself, Jeannie was penning hits for other artists such as Dottie West, Connie Smith, Faron Young, Willie Nelson and Ray Price.

A near fatal automobile accident in 1977 did not slow her down. In recent years the singer, songwriter and record producer has added stage actress and author to her list of accomplishments. In 1988 Jeannie released her self-published book *Pieces of a Puzzled Mind* which now is in its second printing.

That same year she starred as Miss Mona in the Circle Players' production of "The Best Little Whorehouse in Texas" at the Tennessee Performing Arts Center in Nashville. In 1990, although she cracked two ribs in rehearsal, she performed her first straight comedy role in a Nashville area dinner theater's production of "Everybody Loves Opal."

When she isn't touring around the world, fans will find her performing regularly on the Grand Ole Opry on WSM Radio—still at 650, Jeannie's favorite spot on the dial.

RICKY VAN SHELTON

Ricky Van proudly displays an armful of "TNN Music City News Country Awards" selected by Country Music fans.

June has been a very good month for Ricky Van Shelton. On June 19, 1986, he was offered a recording contract with CBS Records. Exactly one year later on June 19, he had his first Top 10 hit and the next day was invited to perform for the first time on the Grand Ole Opry. On June 10, 1988, he became a member of the Grand Ole Opry.

Ricky, who started using his middle name, Van, to avoid being confused with another Ricky Shelton in his native Grit, Va., that night told the audience that he always dreamed about having a big bus and a record deal and hearing himself on the radio. "And I dreamed about playing on the Grand Ole Opry," he added, "but one thing I never dreamed is that I'd be asked to join."

While pursuing his dream to become a country music star, Ricky worked as a pipefitter, appliance store manager, car salesman, construction worker, house painter and grocery store clerk.

All that changed with the release of his first CBS/Columbia album, *Wild-Eyed Dream*, which produced five hits. Besides the title song, it contained the Top 10 hit "Crime of Passion"; and three consecutive No. 1 hits, "Somebody Lied," "Life Turned Her That Way" and "Don't We All Have The Right."

His debut album went to No. 1 on the charts, earned platinum status and led to across-the-board newcomer awards. Ricky was named Top New Male Vocalist by both the Academy of Country Music and *Billboard* magazine, was voted Favorite Newcomer in The Nashville Network's Viewers' Choice Awards, won the *Music City News* Star of Tomorrow award and the Country Music Association's Horizon Award.

His second album, *Loving Proof*, also went platinum and spawned three more No. 1 singles, "I'll Leave This World Loving You," "From A Jack To A King" and "Living Proof." The LP led to eight awards including the CMA Male Vocalist award in 1989.

RVS III, his third album, was certified gold one month after its release, stayed at No. 1 for nine weeks straight on the album charts and yielded three No. 1 singles, "Statue Of A Fool," "I've Cried My Last Tear For You" and "I Meant Every Word He Said" and the No. 2 hit "Life's Little Ups And Downs."

Ricky has since recorded the following albums: *Backroads, Don't Overlook Salvation, Greatest Hits Plus,* and *A Bridge I Didn't Burn.* In 1992, he wrote and published *Tales From A Duck Named Quacker,* the first in a series of children's books.

The Opry star won his first Entertainer of the Year honor and was named Male Artist of the Year during the fan-voted TNN Music City News Awards in, you guessed it, June of 1990. Now it's wait and see what's in store for Ricky Van Shelton whenever June rolls around.

*Jean is flanked by her band, "The Second Fiddles."
Left to right: Jerry Ray Johnston, Glen Dickerson,
Ricky Langston, Robert Crigger and Dave Robbins.*

To be called a legend in the music industry, one must be a pioneer and accomplish many firsts. Jean Shepard has done that. She starred on the first weekly network Country Music Show, "The Ozark Jubilee," she was the first female in Country Music to sell a million records, the first Country Music female vocalist to overdub her voice on record, the first to make a color TV commercial, and the first female Country singer to be with the Grand Ole Opry over 35 years. Jean was born in Paul's Valley, Oklahoma, and spent most of her early life in Visalia, California. She was one of ten children, and Jean says that they were all musically inclined. Music has always been a very important part of Jean's life and so it wasn't surprising that when she was fourteen years old she came up with the idea of forming an all girl western swing band that was called "The Melody Ranch Girls." Jean sang and played string bass and it didn't take long to recognize that this group was good. Soon they were playing for dances and making radio appearances.

One night, "The Melody Ranch Girls" were playing on the same show with Hank Thompson and he was so impressed with Jean's talent that he introduced her to several record executives. Hank was personally responsible for Jean's receiving her first contract on a major recording label. Jean, at fifteen, had her first record and was well on her way to a professional music career. Later she moved to Springfield, Missouri to join Red Foley and the other stars on the Ozark Jubilee. As her fame grew, she felt there was only one place for her to continue her career and she moved to Nashville and was asked to join the Grand Ole Opry in 1955.

Now, many hits later, Jean is a true veteran in the Country Music business. She has recorded twenty-five albums and ten of them are currently available in record shops across the country. Some of the songs that made Jean famous are "Satisfied Mind," "A Dear John Letter," "Forgive Me John," (both million sellers on which she co-starred with Ferlin Husky), "Another Lonely Night," "With His Hand In Mine," "I Want You Free," "Then He Touched Me," "Seven Lonely Days," "Slipping Away," "At The Time," "I'll Do Anything," "Tips Of My Fingers."

With so many hit records behind her, Jean's career is at its peak. Her nomination for the Grammy Award for the "Best Country Female Vocal Performance of the Year" showed the world that Jean Shepard's greatest successes are yet to come.

Jean is married to Benny Birchfield, a musician, singer, and prominent member of Nashville's music community. Together, with their versatile band, "The Second Fiddles," they tour extensively throughout the United States, Canada, and Europe.

A stage full of Country Music and Bluegrass greats! From left on banjos, Sonny Osborne and Earl Scruggs; Jim McReynolds; on mandolins, Jesse McReynolds, Buck White, Bobby Osborne and Bill Monroe; Ricky Skaggs; Sharon White; Patty Loveless and Cheryl Warren.

Although Ricky Skaggs has been a member of the Grand Ole Opry since May 15, 1982, his first encounter with the venerable program—other than as an avid radio listener in his hometown of Cordell, Ky.—came much earlier.

In 1959, at a Kentucky concert by the Opry's Bill Monroe, the Father of Bluegrass, the audience requested that five-year-old Ricky be brought on stage to perform. He played "Ruby" on Monroe's mandolin and received a standing ovation—the first of many throughout his career.

Since that first appearance on stage with Bill Monroe, Ricky Skaggs has performed with some of the giants in the music industry, including Lester Flatt and Earl Scruggs, Ralph Stanley and the Clinch Mountain Boys, pop star James Taylor, Dolly Parton, Emmylou Harris and many others.

A "Triple threat" talent, Ricky has received acclaim for his singing, musicianship and production skills and also for his arrangements on Emmylou Harris' widely praised *Roses in the Snow* album in 1980.

Ricky co-produced (with Steve Buckingham) his album, *Kentucky Thunder*, his ninth LP for Epic. He also produced Dolly Parton's country-comeback album, *White Limozeen*, released in 1990.

He has been honored in more tangible ways with dozens of major music awards in the past 10 years, including the coveted Country Music Association (CMA) Entertainer of the Year award in 1985. Other honors include the CMA Male Vocalist of the Year and Instrumentalist of the Year awards, NARAS (Grammy) award for Best Country Instrumental Performance, TNN Music City News Country Awards Instrumentalist of the Year and Academy of Country Music Touring Band of the Year award.

He also shared a 1987 CMA Vocal Duo of the Year award with his wife, Sharon White, a member of The Whites, another Opry act.

Along with awards, Ricky Skaggs has amassed a string of hit records, including nearly a dozen that reached the top of the charts. "Heartbroke," "Highway 40 Blues," "Honey (Open That Door)," "Cajun Moon," "Crying My Heart Out Over You," "Uncle Pen" and "Lovin' Only Me" are just a few of his No. 1 hits. "Uncle Pen" was the first bluegrass tune recorded by a solo artist to hit No. 1 on Billboard's country chart. And the video of "Country Boy," another No. 1 song, is regarded as a classic.

Although he maintains a full touring and recording schedule, Ricky Skaggs always is able to find time to appear on the Opry.

"To me, traditional music and the Grand Ole Opry have a value in it, a wholesomeness and warmth that some of the other kinds of music don't have. It's our heritage, our roots. It's everything that we're about," he says. "The Opry spirit and music is very, very special."

THE MELVIN SLOAN DANCERS

Since 1952 the Sloan name has been synonymous with middle Tennessee style Square Dancing at the Grand Ole Opry. Ralph Sloan and The Tennessee Travelers began this tradition. Since Ralph's death in 1980 his brother Melvin continues the tradition with The Melvin Sloan Dancers. Throughout these many years, the Sloans' dedication to this unique form of art and entertainment has been such that they have never missed a scheduled performance at the Grand Ole Opry.

The Sloan Dancers perform the unusual Appalachian style of square dancing which is almost unheard of outside of middle Tennessee except by audiences who have seen it performed on the Grand Ole Opry, on television, or in one of the group's many personal appearances. This form of square dancing is a part of the heritage of middle Tennessee. "Dancing From The Heart" is an appropriate definition of this form of dance. In 1980 the Tennessee State Legislature recognized this unique style of square dancing by designating it as the state dance.

The Melvin Sloan Dancers "high energy" performance generates to the audience the feeling of electricity and excitement. The hand-clapping, foot stomping, hard driving rhythm of the dance delights people of all ages. Many of the Opry artists can be seen offstage watching the dancers "do their stuff." This is considered one of the highest compliments any performer can receive.

No other square dance group in the world has reached the level of achievement that the Sloan Dancers have . . . more than 5,000 Grand Ole Opry performances . . . four hundred television appearances . . . including The Today Show .

The Dolly Parton Show . . . 60th Anniversary Of The Grand Ole Opry . . . Hee Haw . . . the first nationwide PBS telecast of the Grand Ole Opry . . . Yesteryear In Nashville . . . Backstage At The Opry . . . TNN's Grand Ole Opry Live . . . several appearances on Nashville Now, the most recent "A Salute to the Grand Ole Opry's 65th Birthday" . . . 16 years as cast member of That Nashville Music, a syndicated TV show aired all over the world.

The Melvin Sloan Dancers were invited in 1983 by President Ronald Reagan to perform at the prestigious John F. Kennedy Center for the Performing Arts in Washington, D.C. in a special salute to the "King of Country Music," Roy Acuff.

Melvin poses backstage with members of the Opry Square Dance Band: Earl White and Lewis Crook, center. Lewis has been performing on the Opry since 1926.

In 1989 the Country Music foundation recognized Ralph Sloan's contribution to the Country Music Industry by inducting him into the Walkway of Stars at the Country Music Hall of Fame in Nashville.

In 1990 Melvin Sloan's dancing shoes and costume along with "An Overview of Square Dancing at the Grand Ole Opry" were presented to the Country Music Foundation in a special ceremony held at the Country Music Hall of Fame during the week celebrating the 65th birthday of the Grand Ole Opry.

Thus the Tradition of Sloan Square Dancing continues into the 90s. And as in the past, the dancers are eagerly waiting for the music to begin, the curtain to rise and the bright lights to flood the stage so that once again they can demonstrate to the world their love of Square Dancing.

Connie lends her own special styling and sound to an Opry favorite.

Connie Smith remembers as a five-year-old saying, "Someday I'm gonna sing on the Grand Ole Opry." She didn't say it too seriously because she didn't think her dream would come true.

The Elkhart, Ind., native was a housewife and mother of a four-month-old son living in Warner, Ohio, in 1963 when she began to realize that dream.

While visiting Frontier Ranch, a park near Columbus, Ohio, Connie was talked into entering a talent contest. She won. Bill Anderson, who was performing at the park that day, heard and met her. Six months later when Connie and her husband attended Anderson's show in Canton, Ohio, they talked again, and he invited her to Nashville.

In March 1964, Connie found herself backstage at the Ryman Auditorium and later sang on Ernest Tubb's "Midnight Jamboree." Two months later she was back in Nashville doing demonstration records of several Bill Anderson songs, and in June, Anderson called to tell her Chet Atkins wanted to sign her to an RCA Victor recording contract.

In July Connie cut her first record, "Once A Day," written by Anderson. It was released in August. By November it was No. 1 on the country charts where it remained for two and a half months.

That same month Connie made her Opry debut. She was visiting backstage again when Loretta Lynn invited her to sing harmony on one of Lynn's numbers. After that Connie, who *Billboard* magazine named Most Promising Country Female Singer in both 1964 and 1965, made numerous guest appearances on the Opry.

More Top 10 hits followed along with guest appearances on major country music television shows. Connie's albums on various labels included both country and religious songs and were highly successful.

Although she had performed regularly on the Opry since 1965, Connie's growing career took her away from the show. Later she took time off from her singing career to devote time to her family, which included two boys and three girls. She rejoined the Opry cast as a member in 1971.

Connie still tours and performs regularly on the Opry. She also makes time for her family which now includes two grandchildren.

Currently she is spending time in the recording studio working on another number one hit.

Dolly Parton put it best when she said: "You know, there's only three real female singers in the world: Streisand, Ronstadt and Connie Smith. The rest of us are only pretending."

Fans who hear Connie Smith sing on the Grand Ole Opry these days agree.

Mike shares a laugh and an autograph with a fan.

"Boy, this feels like home," thought Mike Snider the first time he walked on the stage of the Grand Ole Opry to perform.

The fact that 2,000 residents of his hometown, Gleason, Tenn., were in the audience applauding him on that night in 1984 may have contributed to this feeling.

Six years later, the banjo-playing country comedian and "Hee Haw" regular found a second home at the Grand Ole Opry when the Queen of Country Comedy Minnie Pearl, calling him one of her "dear, dear friends," inducted him into the Opry family on June 2, 1990.

Mike is one of the younger cast members of the Opry. His youth is apparent when he is asked about his first remembrances of the show. While most people say they listened to the Opry on the radio, Mike recalls lounging on the floor in front of the television set and watching it.

"I never thought about getting on it, let alone be a member of it," he added.

Mike, who got his first banjo for his 16th birthday shortly after hearing a Flatt and Scruggs album, has made numerous guest appearances on the show since his memorable debut on Jan. 21, 1984.

A former Mid-South Banjo Playing Contest winner and Tennessee State Bluegrass Banjo champion, Mike was invited to perform on the Opry at that time after winning the National Bluegrass Banjo Championship at age 23.

Fellow Gleason native Gordon Stoker of the Jordanaires and others got the Grand Ole Opry to invite the talented young musician to play. The Opry also invited the entire town of Gleason to attend and the 2,000 home folks gave Snider four standing ovations during his first Opry performance.

In addition to his banjo playing, Snider's down home way of talking caught on with audiences and launched his career as a country comedian. He has made over 100 appearances on TNN: The Nashville Network's "Nashville Now" show.

In the fall of 1987 he became a regular cast member of "Hee Haw." In 1989 he was host of TNN's "Fairs and Festivals" series and did six more TNN specials. In addition to opening for various country music artists, he speaks and entertains at concerts, banquets and conventions across the nation, and is a regular at Opryland USA Entertainment Park.

The country boy who practiced his banjo playing in the mornings before the school bus came and in the afternoons before feeding the hogs has recorded two albums, *Mike Snider and Friends* and *Mike Snider Live at the Station Inn.*

Mike demonstrated his award-winning skills on the banjo by playing "The Alabama Jubilee" and "The Foggy Mountain Breakdown" for the fans in the Opry House on June 2. There to share his Opry induction that night were his mother and daddy, granny and grandaddy and his wife, Sabrina, who is better known to Snider's fans as "Sweetie."

The rest of the folks from Gleason, Snider said, were back home watching the Opry on television.

While he still calls Gleason, Tenn., home, Mike Snider has found a home away from home at the Grand Ole Opry and Opryland.

Backstage, Opry President Hal Durham, Jean Shepard and Mel Tillis help Hank Snow celebrate his 40th Anniversary with the world famous show.

"I was the victim of a broken home at the age of eight. My parents divorced, separating our family of three sisters and myself, and sending two of my sisters to live in foster homes. Through my mother's second marriage, I inherited a cruel, heartless and ignorant stepfather. When I could no longer tolerate the severe punishment that was handed out by him daily, I shipped to sea as a cabin-boy on ships out of Eastern Canada. At the age of twelve, this was a last resort for survival.

"Since that time, I have faced the world on my own. I have known what poverty means. I know what it means to live in the slums of cities. I know what it is to do a man's work when I was only a young boy. I have never forgotten the abuse I received as a young boy, and now it is only natural that I should have a great interest in the welfare of children. Remember, the future of the world tomorrow depends on today's little children."

The above sentiments prompted Hank, in 1978, to establish the "Hank Snow International Foundation For Prevention Of Child Abuse And Neglect of Children, Inc."

Hank was born in Brooklyn, Queens County, Nova Scotia, Canada. And once when the sea-going fellow returned from one of his trips, he learned his mother had obtained a cheap guitar from a mail order house. This gave the youngster his first try on a stringed instrument.

Not long after this, Hank learned that the late Jimmie Rodgers had been discovered by Ralph Peer, and was already recording for the RCA Victor Company. "The Singing Brakeman," as Jimmie was known, was not only to become Hank's

idol, but would serve as his guiding star along the rough road to success. Although Hank worked at many jobs, including work on fish docks, as a stevedore, on farms, etc., he continued his practice on the guitar and often sang to entertain his friends and ward off loneliness. Finally he was encouraged by his friends to seek and audition at Radio Station CHNS in Halifax. He did his first show on the day of his audition.

Soon after acquiring his radio position, Hank decided to form the now famous Rainbow Ranch Boys and established himself as the "Singing Ranger." As Hank matured professionally, more important things came his way. Soon he was invited to become a featured act on the "Canadian Farm Hour." After much persuasion, he was signed to his first recording contract with RCA Victor, Canada, in October of 1936.

In 1949, Hank made his first performing tour in the United States to coincide with the release of his first American record. Hank, who joined the Grand Ole Opry in 1950, has assembled an impressive file of hits, including, "I'm Moving On," "Rhumba Boogie," "Bluebird Island," "Golden Rocket," "Hello Love" and many more. He has recorded more than 80 albums, and more than 2,000 songs and instrumentals.

Hank has received many impressive awards in his lifetime, but still considers citizenship to the United States of America, his involvement with the Hank Snow Child Abuse Foundation, and being an Opry member for over 40 years his greatest rewards.

It is appropriate that country music observers often point to Marty Stuart as the past, present and future of country. He is as progressive an artist as exists today, yet his country roots run deep and wide. He went on the road with Lester Flatt's band when he was 13, startling even veteran pickers with his world-class performances. To understand Marty's ability to merge a variety of styles, one only need hear a story from the days with Lester Flatt.

"One show in particular made a mark on my career," he recalls. "We were playing Michigan State. The opening act was Gram Parsons and Emmylou Harris, then Lester, then the Eagles. That showed me you could play country music and just stand and do what you do. We were Martians to this audience, but they loved us. I never thought I would see country music go to college campuses again, but half the No Hats shows were on campuses and they were sold-out. I feel like a pioneer."

When Flatt died in 1979, Marty branched out, playing a kind of bluegrass fusion with fiddle player Vasser Clements and working with acoustic guitar virtuoso Doc Watson. He also began a six year stint touring and recording with Johnny Cash, which would both leave a lasting impression on the young artist and cause Cash to call Marty his favorite electric guitar player.

The traditional elements of a Marty Stuart performance are to be expected, since the masters of hillbilly music have been a part of the star's life. On stage, he plays country-rock pioneer Clarence White's 1954 Telecaster with a steel guitar-like string bender on the B-string. He also plays a Martin D-45 formerly owned by Hank Williams Sr. and a D-28 that was Lester Flatt's. His bus is Ernest Tubb's old bus, where Marty spent many a youthful hour learning how to play poker from the masters.

Marty Stuart produced his first solo album in 1982 -"Bus Bee Cafe", on the independent Sugar Hill label. The session band on the half-vocal, half-instrumental album attested to the young artist's industry respect: Doc Watson, Merle Watson and Johnny Cash on guitars, Jerry Douglas on dobro, Carl Jackson on banjo. In 1986 he made his major label debut on CBS.

He also became a sought-after session player, with studio and concert credits ranging from

Marty electrifies the Opry fans with another stirring performance.

Willie Nelson, Emmylou Harris, Neil Young and Bob Dylan. (He has since played on sessions for acts such as Randy Travis, Mark O'Conner and the New Nashville Cats, Roy Rogers (vocals), Joy White and Travis Tritt. He continued to hone songwriting skills, and has now had cuts by artists such as Wynonna, George Strait, Emmylou Harris, Joy White and Travis Tritt.

He wrote two songs that became award-winning duets with his friend Travis Tritt: "The Whiskey Ain't Workin" and "This One's Gonna Hurt You". The collaboration on these two songs brought the team a Country Music Association Award for vocal Event of the Year in '92, and "Whiskey" won a Grammy in '93. Their "No Hats Tour" was proclaimed one of the hottest shows on the road in '92—so hot, in fact, that it became the subject of a Pay-Per-View event.

Yet with all the commercial and critical acclaim, Marty's biggest moment came in 1993 when he was inducted as a member of the Grand Ole Opry, upon whose stage he had first appeared as a 13-year-old mandolin-playing teenager.

Every once in a while, Country Music produces an artist who sums up the very best qualities of the sound: sincere, genuine, honest and inspired. Randy Travis is such an artist. The singer, guitarist, and songwriter hasn't been in the national spotlight long, but he's already attracted the king of success and acclaim reserved for artists with three times his tenure.

For Randy Travis, the guiding vision has been a simple one: sing the best country songs available in the most sincere manner possible. The philosophy has led to multi-platinum sales of his first four albums, success on the pop as well as country charts, appearances on TV shows from Carson to Letterman to Saturday Night Live, and spreads in everything from *People* to *Time* to *The New York Sunday Times Magazine*.

In the process, Randy has become a regular feature on record and CD shelves in households that normally don't listen to Country Music, and he's pulled in an audience that includes screaming, sighing girls on his sold-out tour dates.

All this without hip-swiveling or smoke bombs. What Randy Travis does is stand there and sing. That, though, is like saying Marcel Marceau just moves around a little, for Randy's voice and presence convey the combination of tender and tough that have always made country singers attractive and believable.

And there is the wayward background you find so often in the country greats. Randy's teenage brushes with the law nearly landed him a prison term, but he was given instead a chance at what turned into a ten-year apprenticeship at the hands of manager/wife, Lib Hatcher.

And the voice, of course, is the main attraction. "That is a voice that comes along maybe once in a generation," said Minnie Pearl. The comparisons with George Jones and Merle Haggard have been as commonplace as the re-telling of his storybook journey: singing professionally as a child, the turbulent, rebellious teen years, legal scrapes, the link-up with Lib Hatcher, the days as a cook/dishwasher/singer in a Nashville nitery until finally he landed a major label deal. And the comparisons here are dead on target, for to hear Randy turn a melodic phrase is to hear a master at work.

Randy's list of Country Music hits would fill

Randy, Alan Jackson and Opry President Hal Durham meet backstage after Randy introduced Alan as a member of the Opry family.

pages. A few are: "Heroes and Friends," "He Walked On Water," "Hard Rock Bottom Of Your Heart," "Just A Matter Of Time," "Deeper Than The Holler," "Honky Tonk Moon," "Too Gone, Too Long," "Forever and Ever, Amen," "On The Other Hand," "Diggin' Up Bones," and "Point of Light." He has won awards from: The Academy of Country Music; The Country Music Association; TNN/Music City News; The People's Choice Award; Billboard #1 Album Award; Amusement Business Top Grossing Country Touring Artist; AMOA Jukebox Artist of the Year; and a Grammy for Best Country Vocal Performance. Randy became a Grand Ole Opry member in 1986.

Finally, his success has as much to do with his attitude as his music. Country fans will take a lot of things before they'll take phoniness, and Randy has a down-home sincerity they can feel. "This was what I was singing from the first day I started singing," he says. "I can honestly say I never tried to make believe that I am something I am not." That is precisely the attitude that has won him fans both inside and outside Country Music.

Porter Wagoner welcomes a happy Travis Tritt into the Opry family.

From the very beginning, the 1991 Country Music Association Horizon Award winner has been a refreshingly different sort of country artist. Travis Tritt's blend of honky tonk balladry, Southern Rock rowdiness and melodic songwriting is as individual as it is easy to like.

"We're trying to break down the barriers between different kinds of music," Travis says. "I'm a firm believer that there's only two kinds of music: good and bad. I like to describe my music as a triangle. On one side is a folk influence from people like James Taylor, Larry Gatlin and John Denver. On the second side is George Jones and Merle Haggard: that type of music. And then on the third side is The Allman Brothers and The Marshall Tucker Band. They're all balanced together, all a part of what I do."

Travis describes his career thus far as "overnight success that took eight and a half years to happen." Born and raised in Marietta, Georgia, he followed the classic country road of having begun his musical career as a soloist in the children's choir at the neighborhood church. Teaching himself guitar at the age of eight, he wrote his first song at 14.

Upon graduation from high school in 1981, Travis went to work loading trucks and within four years had worked his way up to a management position. Still, he continued to wonder if he had the talent to make it in country music. Not wanting to end up being someone who would always believe he "could have been a contender," he quit his job and began playing solo at any club that would have him.

Travis came to the attention of Danny Davenport, a local representative of Warner Bros. Records. At first, Davenport's interest in Travis was simply as a writer, but once he began seeing him perform in front of an audience, he saw his potential as an artist as well.

When Ken Kragen—best known as the manager of Kenny Rogers and organizer of "We Are The World"—signed Travis as his first entry-level act in more than 20 years, the winning team was complete. Travis' first single, "Country Club," was released in November '89 and reached #9 (*Billboard*) and #13 (*Radio & Records*). This was followed by "Help Me Hold On," which topped the charts in both publications. "I'm Gonna Be Somebody" (#22 *BB*, #1 *R&R*), "Put Some Drive In Your Country" (#28 *BB*, #20 *R&R*), and "Drift Off To Dream" (#3 *BB*, #1 *R&R*), kept Travis' profile high on the charts.

The first single off the album "It's All About To Change," "Here's A Quarter (Call Someone Who Cares)," hit #2 in *BB* and #1 in *R&R* followed by "Anymore" which hit #1 in both *BB* (2 weeks) and *R&R*, *The Gavin Report* and *Cash Box*. His third #1 hit, "The Whiskey Ain't Workin'," pairs him with fellow Grand Ole Opry star Marty Stuart. Travis joined the Opry cast in 1992.

On the road, Travis has confirmed his reputation as a dynamic live performer over and over again. Playing some 280 shows a year, he's developed a crowd-pleasing act that displays the full spectrum of his music. A singer/writer of impressive range and conviction, his music is changing country for the better.

This rare photo taken at the Ernest Tubb Record Shop on Broadway in downtown Nashville, shows E. T. with his daughter Elaine and son Justin. (circa 1954)

Many people don't realize that Justin Tubb, first-born son of the legendary Ernest Tubb, has himself been a member of the Grand Ole Opry for over 35 years. He joined the show in 1955 at the age of 20, which makes him the youngest male regular member ever. Justin was also the first (and until 1984, the only) second generation artist to join the long running show.

Besides his talent as a singer-entertainer, Justin is an accomplished songwriter, having won six B.M.I. awards. His best known works include "Lonesome 7-7203," which has hit three times: in 1963 for Hawkshaw Hawkins; in 1973 for Tony Booth; and in 1983 for newcomer Darrell Clanton. Other successful songs are, "Love Is No Excuse," "Keeping Up With The Joneses," "As Long As There's A Sunday," "Take A Letter, Miss Gray," and his ode to traditional country music, "What's Wrong With The Way That We're Doin' It Now?." After close to ten years, it's still his most requested song.

Though his writing has been mainly for his own recordings in the past few years, Justin is cranking it up again, as well as reactivating the two publishing companies he worked on with his father.

His album, in tribute to his dad, also keyed the birth of a new publishing venture, Troubadour Two Music.

Of his MCA/DOT album, Justin says, "I'm prouder of this album than anything I've ever done in over 35 years in Country Music." The highlights of the album are the three songs Justin wrote just for the album, in memory and tribute to his father; "Sing Blue Eyed Elaine Again," "Just You And Me, Daddy" and "Thanks, Troubadour, Thanks."

Justin continues to carry on with the Midnight Jamboree, Live! from the Ernest Tubb Record Shop, following the Opry every Saturday night. Another great interest for Justin is "F.O.R. E.T." This is a memorial fund, set up with the American Lung Association of Tennessee; to fight emphysema, in his father's name. "F.O.R. E.T." (For Ongoing Research and Emphysema Treatment) has so far collected over $35,000, due mainly to Radiothons.

Any spare time Justin has is spent going to ballgames (baseball mainly), and playing with his VCR. Justin has built quite a library of movies and Country Music shows.

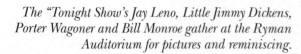

PORTER WAGONER

The "Tonight Show's Jay Leno, Little Jimmy Dickens, Porter Wagoner and Bill Monroe gather at the Ryman Auditorium for pictures and reminiscing.

Sitting around playing guitar and singing during store working hours would not appear to be a good way for a young grocery store clerk to remain in his boss' good graces. For young Porter Wagoner, however, it proved to be his ticket into show business.

When business was slow in the West Plains, Missouri grocery in which Porter was employed, he'd drag out his guitar and sing for whoever cared to listen. The owner of the market enjoyed Porter's singing and decided to sponsor a 15-minute, early-morning local radio show to showcase the talent of his young clerk—and perhaps bring some additional business to the store.

Following that chance beginning, (in the fall of 1951), Porter landed a weekly spot on KWTO Radio in Springfield, Missouri. A few months later, the Ozark Jubilee was born at the station with Red Foley as its director. Red taught Porter many of the lessons of showmanship that were to be so instrumental in Porter's later success, and Porter was soon the feature singer on the nationally televised edition of the show

In 1955, RCA Records signed Porter to a recording contract. Porter's release, "A Satisfied Mind," reached the Number One spot and was followed by a long string of hit records, spanning over 30 years. In 1957, Porter was invited to join the Grand Ole Opry. His long-running syndicated TV series began in 1961. In 1967, Porter auditioned a young singer named Dolly Parton, and she soon became his singing partner. By 1969, the duet had won a Grammy Award for the single "Just Someone I Used To Know." They were named the

Country Music Association's "Duo Of The Year," three years in succession. That partnership lasted until 1974, at which time Porter became involved in producing other artists in his own recording studio, adding new dimensions to his music by branching out into the noncountry musical forms of disco, soul and pop.

When Porter's name is mentioned, images instantly emerge of the tall man with the big smile and the flashy costumes. Porter Wagoner is a Country Music star in the truest sense of the word and he fulfills everything that such a definition entails. As a showman on stage, he is without equal, for he is not merely a singer, but an entertainer par excellence. He has the rare talent of making each person in the audience feel that Porter Wagoner is performing for him alone. It is this unique quality which has made him beloved by persons of all ages and backgrounds. The magic of his show is an outgrowth of Porter Wagoner the man, a person with a good sense of humor and a quiet country charm.

Porter's biography: *A Satisfied Mind: The Country Music Life of Porter Wagoner,* is an outstanding American biography that takes readers behind closed doors to the real world of Country Music, with abundant photos from Porter's personal collection.

Occasionally, when his schedule gets a bit too hectic, Porter heads "out to the lake" to get some rest. Rest, to Porter, consists of non-stop fishing. The evidence of his recreation is some very spectacular bass trophies on the walls of his office.

Billy Walker is pure country—an honest-to-gosh downhome good ole boy—and that's just what he wants to be. Among the current crop of pop- and rock-country crossovers, he's the genuine article, and one of Country Music's most outspoken crusaders for a return to *real* Country Music. The pre-60's *Cheatin' Heart* kind that has spoken to the basic feelings in all of us for years, over the plaintive wail of a steel guitar.

When it comes to "what it's all about," The Tall Texan knows whereof he speaks. Born in Ralls, Texas—a wide spot in the road about 35 miles east of Lubbock "where the chickens chase the jackrabbits"—Billy was one of eight children and went through the Great Depression with no chance to see anything of the world except the several small towns they lived in during that time, ending up in one called Whiteface. When he was thirteen his Dad gave him a dime to see a Gene Autry movie, and that movie set the pattern for Billy's lifelong love—Country Music. He knew then that music was to be his career, and started on the unwavering path that has led him to his present status in the country music world.

With some money earned plucking turkeys for his uncle, Billy bought an old guitar and a 25-cent instruction book, learned at least one new chord from every "picker" that came to town, and soon taught himself how to sing and play well enough to win a radio talent contest in Clovis, New Mexico while he was still in high school. The prizes were $3.00, a chocolate cake, and weekly (unpaid) appearances on a 15-minute radio show. This was a real break, despite the fact that for two years he had to hitchhike the 180-mile trip between Whiteface and Clovis every Saturday to do the radio shows.

After high school Billy travelled with a Texas band, has his own trio for a time, and in 1951 became a member of the Big D Jamboree in Dallas. That same year he signed his first recording contract, which started a long list of over 100 sides, 32 Top Ten hits, and six Number One hits with which he is now identified, such as *Cross the Brazos at Waco, Word Games, Charlie's Shoes,* and *When a Man Loves a Woman.*

From the Big D Jamboree Billy moved on to the Louisiana Hayride, joining newcomers Elvis Presley and Webb Pierce on that prestigious show.

Billy Walker shares a laugh, an autograph, and a video during the annual Fan Fair festivities.

This led to a long stint with Red Foley's Ozark Jubilee, and that in turn led to Nashville in the form of a standing invitation to appear on the Grand Ole Opry, which he joined in 1960. In addition to the Opry, tours around the world, club engagements, and shows at every major arena in the USA, Billy has been seen by millions on TV's Hee Haw, Ozark Jubilee, Pop! Goes the Country, Nashville On the Road, and all of the foremost talk shows. He has entertained more millions at fairs, rodeos, and expositions throughout the country, and still looks forward to each new town and each new audience.

With his big, 6-foot 3-inch frame, easy movements, and congenial personality, Billy is The Tall Texan in every respect. He loves his work, he loves his audiences, and he's never too rushed to stop for another autograph or a word with someone who wants to chat a spell.

People are anxious to come out to see the man whose songs have become so familiar to them on the Opry broadcasts or their stereos. *Billboard Magazine* has listed him as one of the top 20 "most played" artists of the past 20 years, and his *Funny How Time Slips Away* was just recently certified by BMI for a million airplays. Everyone can relate to Billy, just as he relates to them.

If it's Country Music at its authentic best, then it's Billy Walker, the Tall Texan.

As his friends and business associates already know—and as his fans find out wherever Charlie appears—this grey-haired, brown-eyed entertainer is a good natured, easy-moving, personable guy who knows what country music is all about.

Charlie was born in Copeville, Texas. He grew up on his parents cotton farm in Nevada, Texas about 35 miles north east of Dallas. Charlie's father was a Texas lawman and Justice of the Peace. He also taught young Charlie his musical foundation. The Walkers moved to Dallas when he was a senior in high school and Charlie finished school there.

His musical career actually began while still a senior in high school. Charlie got a job singing in a Dallas honky tonk and soon became a vocalist for Bill Boyd's big western swing band, the "Cowboy Ramblers." He was with them for a year until he was called into military service and served two years. One year was spent in Japan where he introduced Country Music to the Japanese people on Armed Forces Radio Network from Tokyo. When he came out of military service he moved to San Antonio, Texas and became one of the nation's top 10 Country disc jockeys.

His first noise making recording was "Tell Her Lies and Feed Her Candy." This was soon followed by his million selling record "Pick Me Up On Your Way Down." He has recorded 35 albums and had 47 songs in the national charts. Some of his other big hits are "Don't Squeeze My Sharmon," "Little Ole Wine Drinker Me," "Truck Driving Man," "My Shoes Keep Walking Back To You," and "Close All The Honky Tonks." Charlie's new album is on M.C.A.

Charlie is at his best in songs that describe the hopes, fears, and problems of everyday people. As an interpreter of country blues he is incomparable. He performs standard country with a deep intensity, while giving a timeless quality to contemporary tunes.

A Grand Ole Opry member since 1967, Charlie has toured every state in the U.S., plus England, Sweden, Germany, Italy, Japan, and Canada. He is a headliner at Las Vegas, Reno, Jackpot and other Nevada cities. Charlie has also chalked up numerous credits via TV guestings on all the leading Country & Western syndicates. In 1981, the Federation of International Country Air

Two famous Texans greet each other backstage, former President George Bush and Charlie Walker.

Personalities (FICAP) inducted Charlie into their Disc Jockey Hall of Fame.

Charlie's hobbies are golf and duck & quail hunting. He shoots golf in the 70s and plays in about 10 pro-celebrity tournaments every year. Some of the tournaments he has played in are the Jackie Gleason Inverarry Classic, The Sahara Invitational in Las Vegas, The Colonial Invitational, The American Cancer Classic, The Southern Open, The Greensboro Open, The Texas Open, The Westchester Classic in New York, and the Atlanta L.P.G.A.

That first professional job at a Dallas honky tonk when he was 17 years old was quite different from the auditorium and packed house engagements he works today. Charlie Walker has come a long way from those early Dallas days, and has proven to be one of America's finest country singers.

Reba McEntire, right, and Rosy, Buck and Sharon White swap road stories backstage at the Opry.

Multi-talented entertainers The Whites have performed as a family for more than 20 years, but they began performing as part of a larger family—the Grand Ole Opry—on March 2, 1984.

With roots in Texas and Arkansas, The Whites come by their country-bluegrass style honestly. And their Christian roots, both in their personal lives and in their music, have added another dimension to the clear, close harmonies that started winning the group fans back in the early 1960s.

Back then, the group included mama Pat White, but the current configuration features Daddy Buck (vocals, mandolin and piano) and daughters Sharon (guitar and vocals) and Cheryl (bass and vocals). Younger daughter Rosie also helps out the group's other instrumentalists.

Following a 1971 move to Nashville, Buck, Sharon and Cheryl started working bluegrass clubs and festivals, and the mid-1980s found them hitting the country charts repeatedly with their clean, acoustic sound.

Some of the group's better-known country hits include "Hangin' Around," "You Put The Blue In Me," "Love Won't Wait" and "Pins and Needles."

Sharon and husband Ricky Skaggs, also a Grand Ole Opry member, won a CMA award for their duet "Love Can't Ever Get Better Than This" in 1987.

In 1988, The Whites released their first all-gospel effort on Word Records. The album, *Doin' It By The Book*, yielded the single "It's Not What You Know (It's Who You Know)," which was chosen for their first video.

"We've never done an album that I've been any more satisfied with and more proud of," Sharon says. "We've done a lot of things that I've felt really good about, but this is the first time I can say that I like every cut equally." Skaggs co-produced the album with The Whites.

This gospel LP helped earn The Whites "Gospel Group of the Year" honors from *Music City News* in 1989.

Although the combination of Country Music and gospel has been performed by many other Grand Ole Opry acts—Roy Acuff, Larry Gatlin and the Gatlin Brothers and the legendary Hank Williams to name a few—probably no act has ever performed it with more feeling than The Whites.

"We just try to do what's right for us," Cheryl says. "Daddy taught us if you treat your music with respect it'll be a good life for you. If you treat it right, it'll treat you right. And if you stay true to yourself, you might not have a number one hit song, but being true to yourself and your music means it'll be right in the end."

TEDDY WILBURN

Del Reeves makes sure he gets his point across to Skeeter Davis and Teddy Wilburn

Teddy Wilburn was just barely six years old, Christmas Eve of 1938, when he and brothers, Lester, Leslie and Doyle and sister, Geraldine, stood huddled together on a corner street in Thayer, Missouri, making their first public appearance. A family musical career that has continued ever since.

"POP" Wilburn had ordered their instruments from the Sears Catalog and rehearsed the children for over a year, inviting neighbors from miles around to come to the Wilburn country home about ten miles from Hardy, Arkansas, for back-yard square dances.

Six month school terms at a one room country schoolhouse left the rest of the year, following their street corner debut, to tour neighboring cities and states, working shows on local radio stations with more street corner appearances as well as school auditoriums, churches, movie houses . . . anywhere their Dad, who acted as manager, agent, and public relations representative could gather a crowd.

Roy Acuff was introduced to their talents in Birmingham, Alabama, and he returned to Nashville, told officials at the Grand Ole Opry about this singing musical group and arranged an audition. The Wilburn Children became regular cast members of the Grand Ole Opry in the spring of 1940, but due to their extreme young ages and the show's late hours, pressures from a child labor organization in those times proved too much for Opry officials and they were forced to terminate the children's stay after only six months.

Returning to small radio stations and working personal appearances continued until sister Ger-aldine got married and left the act. The four brothers continued pickin' and singin' and 1948 found them on The Louisiana Hayride in Shreveport, Louisiana, where they performed until the 1951 Korean conflict took both Teddy and Doyle into active service in Uncle Sam's Army.

After release from service, both Doyle and Teddy went to work with the Webb Pierce Show and were soon back on stage at the Grand Ole Opry. They joined the Opry as regular members in 1953. Webb secured them a recording contract with Decca Records that became a twenty-two year relationship. National and non-country recognition came from appearances on television shows like Arthur Godfrey and Dick Clarks's American Bandstand.

Their own syndicated television show for over twelve years introduced such faces as Loretta Lynn, the Osborne Brothers, Crystal Gayle and numerous other country artists to nation-wide television viewers. Classic Wilburn Brothers recordings; "Trouble's Back In Town," "Roll Muddy River," "It's Another World," "Someone Before Me" and "Arkansas" are evergreen.

On October 16, 1982, The Wilburn Brothers' career ended with Doyles' death by cancer. "It was like a 45-year marriage ended," Teddy said. "There was a lot of adjusting to do."

Teddy Wilburn, a member of the Grand Ole Opry as one of the five Wilburn Children. Then twenty-seven years of sharing the Opry spotlight with Doyle as one of the Wilburn Brothers. Now that same spotlight shines on a crowd pleasing soloist. We hope the name Wilburn and Grand Ole Opry will continue being connected for many more Country Music years.

Being reared on Country Music, freight trains, and hobos could have a definite effect on a young boy. And for one young Texan, those early years would someday be the kind of things legends are made of.

Born in the small town of Sterrett, Texas, Boxcar Willie could rattle off country lyrics before he could even talk in complete sentences. As a two-year-old, Boxcar would run to the door as freight trains traveled less than a stone's throw from his home. It was at this young age that Boxcar began immitating the train whistle as he heard it. He was also delighted by the performances of Jimmie Rodgers, Roy Acuff, Hank Williams and Ernest Tubb as they picked and sang on the family Victrola. His daddy, a railroad man, would fiddle for the family at day's end, passing along pure Country Music rich in Tennessee ancestry.

With a railroad man as the head of the household and a trainyard for a backyard, Boxcar learned a great deal about train hobos. These men taught him a lot with their tall tales and vagabond lifestyles. They would sing, dance, repair things and even fix fancy vittles like rabbit stew.

During his early years Boxcar held many jobs from being a disc jockey to a flight engineer, while still playing his music part time.

In 1976, Boxcar Willie adopted the now-famous hobo attire into his act. It was at this time that Box and his wife "Miz Box" along with the encouragement of their three children, decided that he should devote all of his time to Country Music. In no time at all a love relationship had developed between Box and his ever-growing audiences. Between the tattered cap, weather-worn guitar case and hand-me-down clothes, folks everywhere took a liking to Boxcar's pure country voice and pure gold heart. Not only did things take off in the United States, but his popularity spread like wildfire in England and Scotland.

It is no surprise that the awards started to mount in all three countries. Both *Boxcar Willie* and *Daddy was a Railroad Man* debuted in 1976. What were to follow were more albums: *Boxcar Willie Sings Hank Williams and Jimmie Rodgers*, 1979; *Take Me Home*, 1980; and the popular TV advertised *King of the Road*, 1981; which has sold over 3

America's Favorite Hobo and the Father of Bluegrass Music relax backstage in their dressing room.

million copies; other albums include *Last Train to Heaven, Best of Boxcar Willie, Boxcar Willie, 20 All Time Favorites* and *Not the Man I Used To Be*, which includes his single hit, *"Luther"*. Thus far, Boxcar has 15 Gold albums and four Platinum albums to his credit. During 1978 he collected the International Entertainer of the Year in Great Britain, also in 1978 and in 1979 received the Album of the Year in England. In 1981 Boxcar Willie was honored by the Music City News Awards as Most Promising New Male Artist and became the 60th member of the Grand Ole Opry. In the Country Music Hall of Fame are Boxcar's original hobo hat and coat displayed among Country Music's most outstanding memorabilia. At present, he is writing a book about his life.

More than four decades have passed since those freight trains clammered past his boyhood home, but Boxcar's realistic train whistle has become his trademark.

After makin' tracks across America and Europe and into the hearts of millions, it is no wonder that Boxcar Willie openly declares: "I love America, I love pretty girls, I love Country Music and I love trains." His popularity grows each year and no wonder he's known as "AMERICA's FAVORITE HOBO."

THE VIC WILLIS TRIO

Ronnie Hughes, Curtis Young and Vic Willis rehearse their unique Western harmonies just before their next Opry performance.

The Vic Willis Trio is carrying on a long and famous tradition that began at the Grand Ole Opry in 1946.

Originally known as the "Oklahoma Wranglers," the Willis Brothers—Vic, Guy and Skeeter—began their career at KGEF Radio in Shawnee, Oklahoma. Besides achieving fame in radio, TV, screen and recording, the Willis Brothers had three important firsts in the world of Country Music. . . . the first group to back the late Hank Williams, later becoming known as the original "Drifting Cowboys." . . . the first featured act on the "Jubilee, USA" shows at Springfield, Mo. . . . and they, along with other Grand Ole Opry acts, were the first Country and Western musical entertainers to give a concert in Constitution Hall in Washington, D.C., a place normally reserved for classical music.

With the death of brothers Guy and Skeeter, Vic decided to try a new sound. "I got to thinking, why don't we do something a little different. There was no way we could duplicate the Willis Brothers sound. We could sing the words and music, but it wouldn't be the same at all. Why not try some things we never had time to do as the Willis Brothers."

Vic decided to bring his accordion back out in front as a lead instrument. After that the new Trio spent a great deal of time finding the right songs and arrangements.

The sound was successful from the very first time the Vic Willis Trio performed on the Opry in November, 1979. The Trio performed such established hits as "Old Flames Can't Hold a Candle to You," "If I Said You Had a Beautiful Body," and "The Last Cheaters Waltz," as well as such traditional material as "Shenandoah" and the "American Trilogy," all performed with their own original arrangements.

"It's a sound people say they find unusual, especially the accordion," says Vic. "We've been getting encores at the Opry, and that's the hardest place in the world to get an encore."

Now the Vic Willis Trio is making their niche as one of the freshest harmony sounds in Country Music. But wherever they go, they'll carry with them the spirit and tradition of Guy and Skeeter, the original Willis Brothers.

Country Music is America's music, and the Grand Ole Opry is Country Music's home.

For almost 70 years, the Grand Ole Opry has been entertaining America with a kind of spontaneous, unpretentious, unabashed happening that is unique in broadcasting annals. The Opry music is telling you pieces of life's harsh story. And through it all she is being constantly reminded of Opry founder George D. Hay's first commandment: "Keep her down to earth boys!"

One secret for the Opry's tremendous success is the fact that the show is performed live. Her square-dancers dance and her singers sing. A constellation of stars brighten the audience each show right in front of their very eyes.

Another reason for the Opry's popularity is the illusion that the performance is just happening; that it has no rhyme or reason to it; that it is chaotic informality which somehow stumbles through each weekend.

It is literally true that any single Grand Ole Opry performance will never happen again, but the illusion that the show has not been programmed or planned is not true at all.

The Grand Ole Opry is fortunate to have a capable and dedicated staff responsible for seeing that the world's greatest Country Music show happens 52 weeks a year. This group spends long,

E. W. "Bud" Wendell, President and Chief Executive Officer, Gaylord Entertainment Company.

Dick Evans, Chief Operating Officer and Executive Vice President, Gaylord Entertainment Company.

Hal Durham, President of the Grand Ole Opry and Opryland Production Group.

*Tom Griscom, President of the
Gaylord Communications Group.*

*Bob Whittaker, Vice President and General Manager
of the Grand Ole Opry, directs the Opry operation.*

exacting hours behind the scenes tending to the smallest detail required for a smooth flowing Opry production.

The principal person in charge of shows and other business related to the Opry and its artists is General Manager Bob Whittaker, a Tennessee native. The oldest, most famous Country Music radio show in history appears, at first glance, a manager's nightmare. The Opry is unique in many ways, with its seemingly endless stream of singers and dancers doing their thing, and managing the Opry is a unique experience. There is no other job like it in existence, and there are no schools that teach courses in this business.

"I've thought many times if you sat down to design a successful show, you would probably do everything just the opposite of the way we do," Bob says. "I can't conceive of anybody setting out to pattern a show that has no rehearsals. And we don't know more than 48 hours in advance who is going to be here. We have no advance promotion of the artists you're going to see, and we interrupt the whole thing continually with commercial content." Yet, the Grand Ole Opry actually brings the equivalent of a major convention to Nashville each weekend. Over 850,000 fans attend the Opry shows annually.

*June Rainey keeps a payroll record of each musician
who appears during each Opry performance.*

"The Opry is the ultimate. It is synonymous with being at the top of the ladder, and we can't have off weeks. Each week has to be great," according to Bob Whittaker. "People plan their vacation around the Opry knowing they are going to see the greatest show in Country Music, and we try not to disappoint them. I think of the Opry like I think of the Smithsonian, The Grand Canyon and the Statue of Liberty. It's an American treasure and people travel great lengths to see it." Bob then adds, "And when you get to the end of a Saturday night, sometimes you feel a little apprehensive, because you know that starting next week you have to put it all together again."

The thing that ends in a continuous procession of singers, comics, bands, square-dancers and cloggers on Saturday night does indeed begin Tuesday morning with the delivery of some advertising copy to the desk of a young woman named Becky Jackson at WSM Radio at Opryland. It comes from various advertising agencies, and it is the commercial guts around which the Opry is woven from week to week.

"Each commercial done on the Opry, whether it is done live by the announcers and performers or played on a tape cassette by one of the engineers at the Opry House, must be scheduled beforehand," Becky says. And making up the schedule of commercials and the radio log for every Friday and Saturday night Opry broadcast is the job of Becky and the WSM Traffic Department.

Becky Jackson, of WSM Radio Traffic Department, schedules each commercial announcement and prepares the radio log for the announcers and audio engineers.

The highly professional staff that provides sight, sound, and stageing for the Opry shows is led by Lighting Director, Susan Ray; Audio Engineering Supervisor, Conrad Jones; and Stage Manager, Tim Thompson.

Keith Bilbrey

Hairl Hensley

The Opry announcers play a vital role on every show. They must introduce acts, wave in applause to increase the excitement, read live commercials, and keep a close eye on the clock so that the shows move on schedule. Hairl Hensley, Charlie Douglas, Kyle Cantrell, and TNN's Keith Bilbrey currently perform these duties. During weekdays, all four can be heard over clear Channel WSM Radio AM (650).

Charlie Douglas

Kyle Cantrell

The very first Opry sponsor was Crazy Water Crystal which beamed its message in 1936. Most of the Opry advertisers have been with the show many years. Martha White is the Opry's oldest sponsor having been with the show over 45 years.

Other advertisers on the Friday and Saturday Shows include: Shoney's, Standard Candy, Dollar General Store, Little Debbie Snack Cakes, Sunbeam Bread, Pet Milk, Coca Cola, Cracker Barrel, Randy Travis Enterprises, Rudys Bush Beans, Hamburger Helper, Goody's Headache Powder, Pillsbury, Colgate/Palmolive, Kraft, Chevrolet, Georgia Boot, Tru Value, GHS Strings, Drs. Cream, and Country Music Hall of Fame.

While those sponsors' messages are coming to Becky's desk at radio traffic, Debbie Ballentine, Opry ticket manager, and her staff are busy at Opryland reading the thousands of pieces of mail received there, and answering hundreds of phone calls, and handling Opry ticket requests.

It takes a large, friendly staff to ensure the continued popularity of Opry shows—beginning with the colorful hostesses, ushers, merchandise, and food and beverage personnel who assist those guests entering the front doors, to David Businda and Rosa Mae Hodge, who keep the backstage artists' lounge well supplied with refreshments.

A recent survey indicated that in an average month the Opry Reservations and Ticketing Office will receive ticket requests/information from 50 states, D.C., and 10 foreign countries. This does not include the hundreds of pieces of miscellaneous and artists' fan mail. The Opry fan will travel and comes an average distance of 1,000 miles—round trip—to see the show. Calculations reveal that forty-five percent of the guests come from: Ohio, Illinois, Indiana, Michigan, Tennessee and Wisconsin. It's very convenient and easy to order tickets for the weekend Opry broadcasts or the many matinee performances during the peak season. One can order tickets by phone, mail, or in person at the various ticket outlets sprinkled throughout the Opryland complex. All major credit cards are accepted. To order tickets or request information on show schedules write or call: Opryland USA Reservations and Ticketing, 2808 Opryland Drive, Nashville, Tennessee 37214, (615) 889-6611.

For the Grand Ole Opry's scheduling purposes, Tuesday is really the first day of the week. On that day, Becky begins compiling the advertising copy that arrives at WSM Radio. Debbie and her staff continue to sell tickets, answer phones and mail, and dispense information. At the same time, the Opry Manager's office staff begins contacting the members for appearances on the weekend shows.

Left to right: Clark Cato; Rex England, Maintenance Supervisor; Dallas Morgan; and Phillip Seals keep the Opry House clean and comfortable for its guests.

The person in charge of the preliminary stages is Bob Whittaker's secretary, June Rainey. June calls the talent agents who represent Opry stars. As she inquires about the Opry members, she also gathers information about non-Opry acts who could be available as guests. Normally, Tuesday and Wednesday are required for her to get the necessary information on the members and guests. June averages 450 telephone calls a week. And almost every one is connected with lining up the weekend shows and matinees.

Thursday is the day Bob Whittaker plans his shows. By then, June has completed her list of who's in town and who's out. "She gives it to me and I write out the schedule of sponsors in the order in which their segments come on the Opry shows," Bob explains. "I write down whether the segment is 15 or 30 minutes long. Then I start filling in the names of the acts."

It is not, however, just a matter of writing down names. Some of the Opry's more historic members have, over the years, been afforded certain places on the show by tradition. Hank Snow normally does the 8:30 and 11:00 P.M. shows on Saturday.

One of the finest musical groups in Country Music, the Grand Ole Opry Band. Standing from left to right are: Glen Davis, Buddy Harmon, Joe Edwards, Spider Wilson, Leon Rhodes, Jimmy Capps, Billy Linneman, and Tim Atwood. Seated: Weldon Myrick and Ralph Davis.

Bob will call Debi Hughes—production assistant for the Nashville Network's "Grand Ole Opry Live" show—as soon as he knows what Opry Stars and guest artists will be performing on Saturday at 7:30 P.M. Debi will confer with Director Bill Turner and Associate Producer Janet Tyson. They will decide what artists will appear on the "Opry Backstage" show, and immediately begin promoting the Saturday televised portion of the Opry on TNN.

If there are vacant slots in the schedule after he has filled in all the in-town Opry acts, Bob looks at June's list of available guest artists.

After his tentative schedule is completed Thursday, Bob makes a firmer program on Friday morning to send to the WSM Radio Traffic Department. By early afternoon, the Opry's announcers—Kyle Cantrell, Hairl Hensley, Charlie Douglas, and TNN's Keith Bilbrey—have seen the schedule and know which stars they are to be working with on the segments they are to announce.

The Opry has found its lifeblood in the mingling of old and new entertainers, the living legends and the hot arrivals. More than 20 stars appear on each Friday and Saturday evening show, presenting songs that stretch from Country Music's string-band days to present-day chart-topping hits.

"The Grand Ole Opry will continue to reflect not only the history and traditional type of Country Music, but will also reflect what is current and what is happening in Country Music today," explains Bob Whittaker. "The Opry has always tended to react to what's happening in Country Music. I don't think it's been a trendsetter or a force for change, but it reacts to it," he adds. "And the young fans, especially, are really excited about the new Opry Superstars such as: Randy Travis, Vince Gill, Lorrie Morgan, Alan Jackson, Clint Black, Garth Brooks, Reba McEntire, Holly Dunn, Ricky Skaggs, Patty Loveless, Emmylou Harris, Alison Krauss, Hal Ketchum, Marty Stuart, Travis Tritt and Joe Diffie.

"Because we're able to blend the legends of Country Music with today's stars, I think the future of the Opry is very bright," Bob noted. "But the Opry's future will always be very much related to its rich and colorful history."

It is now Friday evening. The Opry fans from around the world have acquired their tickets, poured in the doors, and are settling into their seats. The stagehands, lighting director, stage manager, engineers, and staff band are poised, waiting for the opening curtain. The Opry star scheduled to MC the first sponsored segment is on stage waiting for the show to begin.

Bob Whittaker is standing in the wings waiting to see how the next show he has constructed is going to be received by the audience in the Opry House or via the radio broadcasts. June Rainey is watching with a clipboard to keep a payroll record of which musicians play instruments on every song.

Everyone is waiting for the same thing—the beginning of another historic show which puts itself together before your very eyes. Then that giant orange curtain rises and you watch the first step in the week-long process of resurrecting the Grand Ole Opry.

For the 4,400 in the Opry House and thousands listening on WSM Radio—it is once again, "Showtime!"

While the Grand Ole Opry show moves briskly along throughout the evening, there is another "show" going on backstage. Early in the evening, performers roam easily from dressing rooms to their metal lockers in the hallways. Backstage, the activity is moving along at a casual, comfortable pace. Artists and friends embrace and inquire genuinely about home and work. Then they begin horsing around and joking. The prominent sound is laughter; the overall tone is warm.

The Opry backstage is noisy and congenial. The atmosphere doesn't so much resemble a show-business gathering as it does a reunion of lifelong friends. The center of all this activity is a large, open foyer near the two rear stage entrances. Known as the green room, it's actually more like a grandmother's spacious living room than the traditional warm-up area included backstage at most theaters. People arrive and depart intermittently, and the constant coming and going fuels an atmosphere rich in gracious greetings, loud laughter and fond farewells.

Throughout the night, singers and musicians drift through the double-wide doors leading from the dressing area to the stage. Although huge clocks are positioned strategically near the stage—this is a live broadcast, after all, requiring certain time cues—the performers don't seem to pay them much attention. For most of the stars, the Opry schedule and pace have been committed to memory. As the minutes to their turn in the spotlight click down, the performers carry on with their talking and teasing. They sign autographs and pose for snapshots. They shake hands with that show's announcer and then, finally, walk on stage as casually as they might stroll through the front door of their own house. Then they smile and wave to the audience, knowing they're home once again, among friends, among family.

It is now a little past midnight—Sunday morning. The crowd has left the Opry House; some bound for the Ernest Tubb Midnight Jamboree; an early breakfast, or their hometowns throughout America. Reverberating melodies follow the Opry stars into the cool darkness. The imposing Opry House is silent again.

But if one listens carefully he can almost hear the remarks Judge Hay delivered at each show's finale…echoing through the empty auditorium:

"That's all for now friends…
Because the tall pines pine
And the pawpaws pause
And the bumblebees bumble all around.
The grasshoppers hop
And the eavesdroppers drop
While, gently, the old cow slips away…
George D. Hay saying, so long for now!"

Visiting Opryland Is Like Playing A Guitar. Just Take Your Pick And Play.

Nowhere in Nashville but Opryland themepark will you find this much exciting entertainment for every member of your family! No matter what your age, you can pick and choose at Opryland and find just what you're looking for. Moms and dads just love our wonderful musical shows that not only feature live country, Broadway, rock and Cajun music, but also debut some of the hottest talent in the country.

The younger set will thrill at our hair-raising roller coasters, skin-drenching water rides and challenging games of skill. We even provide a special children's area complete with rides and shows for the little ones. One thing's guaranteed, everyone has fun at Opryland.

OPRYLAND

So make your family vacation an Opryland themepark vacation! We're open weekends in April, and daily beginning May 6.

FOR MORE INFORMATION CALL 615-889-6611.

With A Name Like Grand Ole Opry, Giving The Best Tours Comes Naturally.

Take it from the people who know Music City! A Grand Ole Opry Tour is the best way to see the best of Nashville. With so many fascinating tour options, it's fun for the whole family! Whatever sights interest you, you'll be sure to enjoy them more aboard one of our comfortable, air-conditioned tour buses. **GRAND OLE OPRY TOURS** Let our trained, highly informed and friendly guides show you the homes of the stars, Nashville's famed Parthenon, the newly renovated historical Ryman Auditorium, the Country Music Hall of Fame, The Hermitage, and more. The only way to do Nashville is on a Grand Ole Opry Tour!

FOR MORE INFORMATION CALL 615-889-6611.

A Property of Gaylord Entertainment Company

{ GRAND OLE OPRY }

Join The Grand Ole Opry Fan Club.

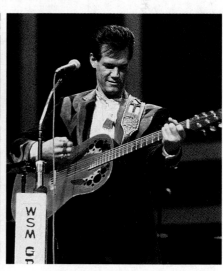

Make it official. Tell the world you're a country music fan by becoming a member of the Grand Ole Opry Fan Club. As a member, you'll receive ❑ A history of the Grand Ole Opry ❑ Personalized membership card ❑ Fan Club button ❑ Official Fan Club bumper sticker ❑ Quarterly newsletter ❑ Special offers and contests for members only. Dues are only **GRAND OLE OPRY** $10 a year in the United States and Canada, and $12 a year for those living overseas. For more information, write the Grand Ole Opry Fan Club, 2804 Opryland Drive, Nashville, Tennessee 37214.

{ F A N   F A I R }

Enjoy Fan Fair! The Only Time Of Year The Stars Stay Out All Day.

Nowhere else do so many top country entertainers come together to meet their fans and sign autographs. Major recording companies keep the stage crackling all week with almost non-stop concerts. And as a Fan Fair registrant, you'll receive a ticket to Opryland themepark, the Country Music Hall of Fame and the Ryman Auditorium. You'll also receive two free lunches and have access to the exhibit area where you'll see the latest in country music recordings and merchandise. To find out cost, dates and how to register, write to Fan Fair, 2804 Opryland Drive, Nashville, Tennessee 37214.

INTERNATIONAL FAN FAIR NASHVILLE, TENNESSEE

COUNTRY MUSIC FAN FAIR ℠

WSM. Three Letters That Stand For Nashville And Country Music.

Every Friday and Saturday night, folks have gathered 'round the radio as the Grand Ole Opry stars gather 'round AM 650 WSM's microphones. Here is where WSM's Grand Ole Opry, the Mother Church of Country Music, was born and blossomed into the world's longest-running radio show. Legendary for its nighttime signal which serves communities within a 750-mile radius, WSM is also the unparalleled source of news and entertainment for Nashville, one of the South's most dynamic cities. So when it comes to Nashville and country music, remember the three letters that say it all. WSM.

The Grand Ole Opry is as simple as sunshine. It has a universal appeal because it is built upon good will, and with folk music expresses the heart-beat of a large percentage of Americans who labor for a living.—George D. Hay, founder of the Grand Ole Opry.

DeFord Bailey

George D. Hay and Uncle Jimmy Thompson—1925

The world famous Grand Ole Opry is a show business phenomenon. This live Country Music radio program has entertained millions of Americans for over 65 years. And it is more popular today than ever before. The Opry's history is rich, colorful and distinguished. Its past is unique as the show itself.

The "Roaring Twenties" were turbulent and exciting years for America and the world. In 1920 the Versailles Treaty went into effect, and the doomed League of Nations was created. War broke out between Poland and Russia. It was a decade that saw Man O'War win the Belmont and Preakness Stakes, the beginning of air mail service between New York and San Francisco, and a young cornetist named Louis Armstrong came from New Orleans to Chicago, joined Joseph "King" Oliver's Creole Jazz Band and made musical history.

George D. Hay—The Solemn Old Judge

The "Possum Hunters"—Front: Walter Leggett, Dr. Humphrey Bate, Buster Bate, Staley Walton. Standing: Oscar Stone and Aaron Albright. The first country band to play on WSM Radio.

The Crook Brothers—Blythe Poteet, guitar; Kirk McGee, fiddle; Bill Etters, guitar; Herman Crook, harmonica; and Lewis Crook, banjo.

"The Fruit Jar Drinkers"—From left: "Grandpappy" George Wilkerson, Claude Lampley, Tommy Leffew and Howard Ragsdale.

The early twenties also saw great developments in the radio field. Before the end of the decade this infant medium would have a profound influence on the social, economic, and entertaining life of the United States.

On November 2, 1920, radio station KDKA in East Pittsburgh, Pa., began the first regular broadcasting service by airing the returns of the Harding-Cox election. The first commercially sponsored program in the United States was broadcast by WEAF New York on May 12, 1922. By 1924, radios in the United States numbered over 2,500,000. Five years earlier there were not more than 5,000 receiving sets in America, and most of these were in the hands of expert technicians. Nowhere was the impressive influence of radio more felt than in Nashville, Tennessee.

One of the really memorable events for the city of Nashville took place on October 5, 1925.

On the evening of that date the first program was broadcast over National Life and Accident Insurance Company's new radio station, WSM. The call letters, reflecting insurance company ownership, stand for "We Shield Millions."

Grand Ole Opry Cast—1927.

The early interest in radio of E. W. Craig, then vice president of the company, had much to do with its decision to enter the broadcasting field. WSM began as a 1,000 watt station—one of only two in the entire South with that much power, which was twice as strong as 85 per cent of all stations in the United States.

"The Gully Jumpers"—From left: Bert Hutcherson, Roy Hardison, Charlie Arrington and Paul Warmack.

Sam and Kirk McGee, "The Boys From Sunny Tennessee."

"Uncle Ed Poplin and His Ole Timers"—Standing left: Jack Woods and daughter, Louise, Ed Poplin. Seated: Frances Woods and Ed Poplin, Jr.

Son Dorris and Uncle Dave Macon, "The Dixie Dewdrop"

That Nashville should be known as "Music City USA" is a result of WSM and the Grand Ole Opry, which have always been the nerve center of the country music industry. For over half a century, the Opry and the radio station have directly influenced the city's economic and physical growth. Without its dedication to country music and its nurturing of talent, it is doubtful the industry would have centered in Nashville.

"Without the Opry, I don't believe we could have had a Music City USA," Craig had said. "It came to be the dream of every folk musician to be on the Opry. It was only a matter of time until 'cowboy laments' and other new songs were written for Opry performers. They became popular, but it meant a complete shift away from folk music. These new songs were popularized on the Opry, then played on the juke boxes around the country. They gave rise to a whole new gamut of country western music with Nashville and the Opry being the musical backbone."

The Opry had its beginning on November 28, 1925, on the fifth floor WSM Studio of the National Life and Accident Insurance Company. Legend has it that the featured performer on

"Jack Shook and the Missouri Mountaineers"—From left: Jack Shook, Dee Simmons, Bobby Castleman, Arthur Smith, and Nap Bastian.

The Delmore Brothers—Rabon, left, and Alton.

Left to right, Robert Lunn, George Wilkerson, Glen Stagner, and minstrel, Lasses White.

Paul Howard, second from left, and his "Arkansas Cottonpickers."

The announcer was one of America's pioneer showmen. George D. Hay, a reporter for the Memphis Commercial Appeal, started his radio career when he was appointed radio editor for the newspaper. He first went on the air over the Commercial Appeal's station, WMC, in June of

Roy Acuff, left, and his "Crazy Tennesseans."

that show was Uncle Jimmy Thompson, an eighty-year-old fiddler who boasted that he could fiddle the "taters off the vine." His early appearance, however, was restricted to one hour, not quite enough time to prove his reputation of knowing a thousand fiddle rounds.

Jamup and Honey

One of the early Grand Ole Opry Tent Shows.

The Bailes Brothers.

Bill Monroe, second from right, and one of his early "Bluegrass Boys" band.

Left, Cowboy Star, Johnny Mack Brown, Pee Wee King and his "Golden West Cowboys."

Eddy Arnold sings to a large war time street crowd in downtown Nashville.

1923. A year later he went to Chicago and was appointed chief announcer of Radio Station WLS. Here he was voted America's most popular radio announcer in a nationwide contest conducted by The Radio Digest. Here, also, he originated the WLS Barn Dance, later to become known as the National Barn Dance.

On October 5, 1925, Hay came to Nashville for the dedicatory ceremony inaugurating WSM. One month later he joined the station as its first director.

Then at 8 P.M. on November 28, 1925, he announced himself as "The Solemn Old Judge" (although he was only 30 years old) and launched the WSM Barn Dance. Two years later he gave it the title "The Grand Ole Opry."

WSM, a member of the National Broadcasting Co. network, was also carrying on Saturday nights "The Music Appreciation Hour" conducted by a celebrated personality, Dr. Walter Damrosch. The Station followed that hour with three hours of "barn dance" music.

Hay later recalled the moment in a 1945 pamphlet. "Dr. Damrosch always signed off his concert a minute or so before we hit the air with our mountain minstrels and vocal trapeze performers. We must confess that the change in pace and quality was immense. But that is part of America—fine lace and homespun cloth.

"The monitor in our Studio B was turned on, so that we would have a rough idea of the time which was fast approaching. At about five minutes

Curly Fox and Texas Ruby before the present era of luxurious, custom made buses.

Whitey Ford, "The Duke of Paducah."

L. to R.: Hank Williams, Milton Estes, Red Foley, Minnie Pearl, Geroge Rosen—Radio Editor of Variety magazine—Harry Stone, Eddy Arnold, Roy Acuff, Rod Brasfield, Lew Childre.

In front: Wally Fowler

Bradley Kincaid

before eight, your reporter called for silence in the studio. Out of the loudspeaker came the correct, but accented voice of Dr. Damrosch and his words were something like this: While most artists realize there is no place in the classics for realism, nevertheless I am going to break one of my rules and present a composition by a young composer from Iowa, who sent us his latest number, which depicts the onrush of a locomotive. . . .

"After which announcement the good doctor directed the symphony orchestra through the number which carried many 'shooshes' depicting an engine trying to come to a full stop. Then

he closed his program with his usual sign-off.

"Our control operator gave us the signal which indicated that we were on the air. We paid our respects to Dr. Damrosch and said something like this: Friends, the program which just came to a close was devoted to the classics. Dr. Damrosch told us that it was generally agreed that there is no place in the classics for realism. However, from there on out for the next three hours we will present nothing but realism . . . It will be down to earth for the earthy.

"In respectful contrast to Dr. Damrosch's presentation of the number which depicts the onrush of locomotives, we will call on one of our performers—DeFord Bailey, with harmonica to give us the country version of his 'Pan American Blues.'

Left: Curly Fox, Zeke Clements and Roy Acuff.

Curley Williams and his "Georgia Peach Pickers."

Chet Atkins and Mother Maybelle, with guitars, and the Carter Family.

Cousin Jody, left, with Lonzo and Oscar.

The York Brothers—George and Leslie.

Hank Williams, a Country Music Legend.

"Whereupon, DeFord Bailey, a wizard with the harmonica, played the number. At the close of it, your reporter said: "For the past hour we have been listening to music taken largely from Grand Opera, but from now on we will present 'The Grand Ole Opry!'"

It wasn't long before the crowds clogged the corridors of the WSM studio to observe the performers. This led to a decision. Edwin W. Craig, the man of early and continuous vision, suggested that all the observers be allowed to watch in a studio so their reactions could add to the program. His suggestion led to the construction of Studio "C," an acoustically designed auditorium capable of holding five hundred enthusiastic fans.

Patsy Cline and Ernest Tubb.

Cowboy Copas and George Morgan

Soon the auditorium-studio could no longer accommodate the throngs, so the search for an appropriate home began. The first move was to the rented Hillsboro Theatre, a former movie house in what was then the southwest part of the city. When the audience continued to grow, Opry officials sought another hall.

A huge tabernacle across the Cumberland River in East Nashville was available. Although the floor was covered with sawdust and the splintery benches were crude, the audience outgrew this location in two years.

In July, 1939, the show moved to the newly-constructed War Memorial Auditorium, an entrance fee of twenty-five cents was imposed in an effort to curb the crowd. It didn't work; the weekly crowds averaged better than 3,000. The move to the Ryman Auditorium in 1943 was a necessity.

The Ryman had been built in 1891 by riverboat captain Tom Ryman who came to a religious tent meeting to heckle the preacher, only to stay and be converted. He built the structure for the Reverend Sam Jones. The Confederate Veterans reunion was scheduled in 1897, and a balcony was added for the meeting. It then could seat more than 3,000 people.

The first real country band to appear on WSM was headed by a genial physician, Dr. Humphrey

Gentlemen Jim Reeves, Jack DeWitt and Del Wood.

Hank Snow and Lew Childre performed for hundreds of servicemen in Korea.

The Louvin Brothers—Charlie, left, and Ira, right, with Faron Young.

Edwin W. Craig, Dizzy Dean and Stringbean

Bate. At the time of Dr. Bate's death in 1936, Judge Hay wrote, "As a matter of fact, Dr. Bate played on the station even before the Barn Dance started." Dr. Bate was a graduate of Vanderbilt University Medical School and played harmonica. He joined the Opry with six of his neighbors and named them the Possum Hunters. At the piano was Dr. Bate's 13 year old daughter, Alcyone, who performed for 50 years each Saturday night. Other outstanding string bands were: The Gully Jumpers, The Fruit Jar Drinkers, The Crook Brothers, Arthur Smith and His Dixie Liner, The Binkley Brothers and their Clod Hoppers, Uncle Ed Poplin and his Ole Timers, The Delmore Brothers, and Jack Jackson and the Bronco Busters.

Uncle Dave Macon, "The Dixie Dewdrop," joined the Opry in 1926 after several years in Vaudeville. He remained its top star for many years.

Until 1938 the Grand Ole Opry placed virtually all emphasis on instruments. There were some singers, but they were subordinate to the band. Then came young Roy Acuff and the Smoky Mountain Boys. A short time later, one of the instrumentalists in the band of Pee Wee King and his Golden West Cowboys stepped forward to sing. That was the start of the career of Eddy Arnold, "The Tennessee Plowboy." Arnold later formed his own group, and the rush was on. Red Foley became a hit, then Ernest Tubb, Cowboy Copas and Hank Williams.

Left to right: Johnny Wright, Carl Smith, Tex Ritter, Webb Pierce, Smilin' Eddie Hill, and Jack Anglin.

Lew Childre at the mike and "Mr. Guitar," Chet Atkins on drums.

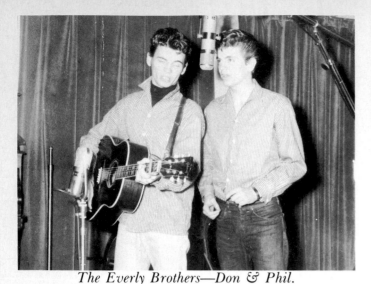

The Everly Brothers—Don & Phil.

Snooky Lanson and Dinah Shore

On came the Duke of Paducah, Whitey Ford. He had been the star of a network radio show "Plantation Party." Then Minnie Pearl and Rod Brasfield, Curly Fox, Texas Ruby and the Fox Hunters. Those were the days of minstrels, and the Opry produced Jamup and Honey. Bill Monroe arrived to introduce Bluegrass Music.

Others included Uncle Joe Mangrum and Fred Schriver, Asher Sizemore and Jimmy, the Vagabonds, Lew Childre, Zeke Clements, Paul Howard, Curly Williams and Clyde Moody.

In 1939, the Opry was carried on the NBC network for the first time. Sponsored by Prince Albert, the first show featured Uncle Dave Macon, Roy Acuff, Little Rachel, the Weaver Brothers and Elviry, and the Solemn Old Judge. This same group made the first Grand Ole Opry movie a year later. The late Vito Pellettieri, Opry stage

Hawkshaw Hawkins

Johnny Cash.

Two members of the Country Music Hall of Fame, Grant Turner and Tex Ritter, answer a listener's call at the WSM Radio studio.

manager since 1934, handled all the complicated stage traffic.

The 1940's and 1950's brought new stars to the Opry: Lester Flatt and Earl Scruggs, Lonzo and Oscar, Ray Price, Johnny and Jack, the Carlisles, Mother Maybelle Carter, Ferlin Husky, the Jordanaires, Stringbean, Cousin Jody, Marty Robbins, Hank Snow, Don Gibson, The Stoney Mountain Cloggers, The Ralph Sloan Dancers, Billy Grammer, Charlie Louvin, Jean Shepard, Little Jimmy Dickens, Justin Tubb, Kitty Wells, The Willis Brothers, Margie Bowes, George Morgan, Bobby Lord, Hank Locklin, Hawkshaw Hawkins, Del Wood, Faron Young, Jim Reeves, Jimmy Newman, Roy Drusky, Johnny Cash, Grandpa Jones, Archie Campbell, The Everly Brothers, Wilma Lee and Stoney Cooper, Porter Wagoner, George Hamilton IV, Skeeter Davis, and the list continues.

The 1960's brought no let-up in new and great talent. They include Marion Worth, LeRoy Van Dyke, Dottie West, Tex Ritter, Bobby Bare, Connie Smith, Bob Luman, Billy Walker, Sonny James, Ernie Ashworth, Loretta Lynn, The Osborne Brothers, Jim and Jesse, The Glaser Brothers, Jim Ed Brown, Jack Greene, Dolly Parton,

Kitty Wells

Earl Scruggs and Lester Flatt

Del Reeves, George Jones, Mel Tillis, Jeannie Seely, Stu Phillips, Charlie Walker, The Four Guys, Ray Pillow and others.

The 1970's and 1980's saw great new talent join the Opry cast. They include Roy Clark, Jerry Clower, John Conlee, Holly Dunn, Larry Gatlin, Tom T. Hall, David Houston, Jan Howard, Patty Loveless, Reba McEntire, Mel McDaniel, Barbara

Ferlin Husky and Vito Pellettieri, who became the Opry's Stage Manager in 1934.

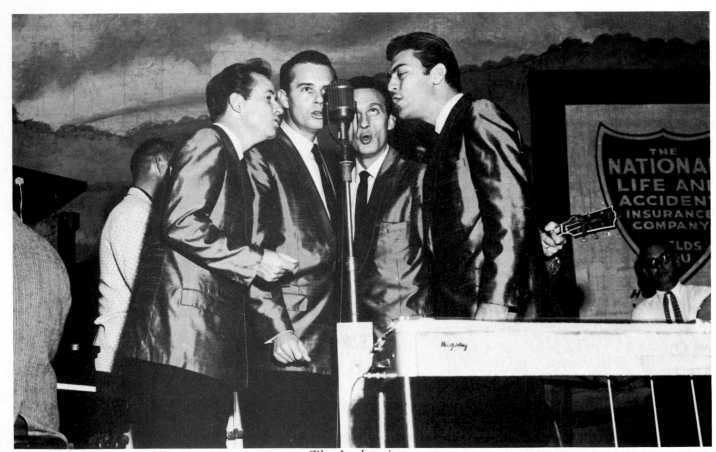

The Jordanaires

Stoney & Wilma Lee Cooper

Bob Luman

Mandrell, Ronnie Milsap, Lorrie Morgan, Jeanne Pruett, Riders In The Sky, Johnny Russell, Ricky Van Shelton, Ricky Skaggs, Connie Smith, Randy Travis, The Whites, and Boxcar Willie. The Opry has since added: Clint Black, Garth Brooks, Mike Snider, Alan Jackson, Vince Gill, Emmylou Harris, Alison Krauss, Charley Pride, Marty Stuart, Travis Tritt, Joe Diffie and Hal Ketchum.

The Grand Ole Opry family is unique. But like every other family it shares many human emotions. It has not always had the happiest of times. Tragedy has been a sad chapter in its history.

In 1953, at the age of twenty-nine, Hank Williams died in the back seat of a car somewhere between Knoxville, Tennessee and Oak Hill, West Virginia. Ten years later, Patsy Cline, Hawkshaw Hawkins, Cowboy Copas and his son-in-law, Randy Hughes were killed in an airplane crash. Then Jack Anglin, Betty Jack Davis, Texas Ruby Owens, Jim Reeves, Ira Louvin and Sam McGee were lost in tragic accidents. Probably the most publicized disaster occured in 1973 when Stringbean and his wife, Estelle, were murdered at their farm after a Grand Ole Opry performance.

From every state in the Union and many foreign countries 900,000 Opry fans annually travel an average of 1,000 miles round-trip to see the Friday, Saturday and Sunday performances. It has been estimated that an additional seven to eight million see Opry stars themselves journey three million miles a year in making these appearances. Today the Nashville Area Chamber of Commerce proclaims the fact that the city's music industry, an offshoot of the Opry, is a billion dollar a year business. The statistics are impressive indeed. Nashvillians are employed by recording studios, record pressing plants, talent agencies, trade papers, recording companies and performing rights organizations. Through the Opry, WSM has created a musical family that has in turn made Nashville "Music City, U.S.A."

March 16, 1974, former President and Mrs. Richard Nixon attended the premiere performance at the new Opry House. Here Roy Acuff tries to help President Nixon learn the art of the Yo Yo. Since that historic initial show, the Opry House welcomed government officials and celebrities from all walks of life. And in June 1976, for the first time in its history, Ambassadors to the United Nations assembled away from their New York headquarters and visited the Grand Ole Opry.

In October 1975, the joint U.S.—USSR Apollo-Soyuz Test Project crew docked on the stage and presented Opry Manager Hal Durham a color photo taken from space showing Opryland along the Cumberland River. Left to right, Cosmonaut Valeriy N. Kubasov, Astronaut Vance D. Brand, Durham, Astronauts Donald K. Slayton and Thomas P. Stafford.

In fact David Cobb, retired WSM personality, is responsible for dubbing the town "Music City" many years ago. The first recording studio, Castle, was put together by three former WSM engineers: Aaron Shelton, George Reynolds and Carl Jenkins. And the man generally considered the father of Music Row's recording industry was Owen Bradley, former musical director of WSM. Bradley succeeded Beasley Smith who penned such famous songs as: "The Old Master Painter from the Faraway Hills" and "Lucky Old Sun."

Bradley was succeeded by Marvin Hughes, who later became a producer for Capital. Hughes' successor was Bill McElhiney, whose successes have included arranging for Danny Davis and the Nashville Brass. Roy Acuff and Fred Rose both worked at WSM. They teamed to form Acuff-Rose, the publishing and talent management empire. Chet Atkins, one of Nashville's musical giants and a key RCA executive, came to WSM as a sideman with the Carter Family. Jack Stapp, who had been program director and produced the old Opry network shows for NBC, formed Tree Publishing Company. Frances Preston, head of BMI, had worked for the station in the promotion department. There was also Dinah Shore, Snooky Lanson, Tennessee Ernie Ford, Phil Harris, Kitty Kallen, James Melton, Francis Craig and Anita Kerr among others.

The body and soul of music is the musician.

In Nashville he has prospered. WSM and the Grand Ole Opry have been patrons of live music for more than six decades. Now there is a boon in Country Music. But even during the long, lean, early years, music was always present in the studios and halls of WSM.

There are performers who have been members of the Grand Ole Opry for 20, 30, and even 50 years. The disbursement of weekly and monthly monies has not been confined to a few. Witness the hundreds of stars and thousands of "sidemen" who have performed on the Opry, and the dozens of staff musicians employed by WSM in the pop field and now, TNN in the television field.

Dottie West

Young Doyle Wilburn and Marty Robbins, right, at the WSM Radio studio with D.J., T. Tommy Cutrer, center.

Continuing in the traditional role of vanguard for new concepts in broadcasting, WSM gave America its first commercial frequency modulation radio station in 1941. Retired WSM President, John H. DeWitt, who manned the audio controls at the first Opry broadcast, was the principal force behind this new venture. W47NV is now a part of broadcast lore, partly because people were uninterested in buying a converter or receiver to pick up the station's signal. In the early sixties, interest in FM revived. WSM-FM (95.5) made its debut in 1968 with 100,000 watts. The station broadcasts in stereo with vertical and horizontal polarization. It covers a 100-mile radius surrounding Nashville.

In 1950, WSM brought Nashville its first television station. The video facility set up a series of five microwave relay stations between this city and Louisville, thereby becoming the first TV network affiliate in town. The station also brought this area its first color programs and installed the first color film processor in Nashville.

March 4, 1978. For the first time in its colorful history, the Grand Ole Opry was televised live over the national PBS Television Network.

WSM's largest influence on the growth and economy of Nashville is the construction of a multi-million dollar family entertainment park and music center. Of course, the Grand Ole Opry House is the focal point of this project.

In the summer of 1968, Irving Waugh, president of WSM, Inc., and National Life executives, Edwin Craig and Bill Weaver, talked of plans to build a new Opry House. When they began thinking in terms of space and parking and other considerations, the plan for a park was conceived.

At the 1968 Grand Ole Opry Birthday Celebration, Waugh announced to the thousands of disc jockeys and music industry notables that a feasibility study would be undertaken to determine if such a complex were economically sound. At the 1969 birthday celebration, Waugh stated that all systems were go.

Opryland USA, a 400-acre theme park, is designed to be "The Home of American Music." The park is divided into entertainment areas that combine live musical shows, restaurants, gift shops, and sensational thrill rides. Opryland opened its gates to the public on May 27, 1972, and the Opry moved to Opryland USA on March 16, 1974, when the 4,400-seat Grand Ole Opry House was completed.

The advent of Opryland USA marked the beginning of a period of rapid growth. An interest in television, begun in 1950 when WSM-TV first

An historic occasion, the purchase of Opryland USA Inc by Gaylord Broadcasting, July 1, 1983. Making the happy announcement on the Opry stage are, left to right, E. W. "Bud" Wendell, Mrs. Thelma Gaylord, Minnie Pearl, Edward L. Gaylord, chairman of Gaylord Broadcasting, and Roy Acuff.

The Opry hits the road again! Minnie Pearl and Ricky Skaggs announce the historic 10-city itinerary for the True Value American Tour.

aired, expanded in 1974 when Opryland Productions began operation. With facilities in the Grand Ole Opry House, Opryland Productions produced shows and commercials for many clients, and it won three Emmy awards for videotape editing for ABC-TV's coverage of the 1976 Montreal Olympics.

In 1975, plans were announced to add a major hotel to Opryland USA. In 1977, the Opryland Hotel opened with 600 guest rooms and a special devotion to meetings and conventions. It added 467 rooms in 1983 and another 824 rooms in 1988. In 1993, Gaylord Entertainment Company announced a massive $175 million expansion to the Opryland Hotel, adding 979 guest rooms. It will be completed in mid-1996 giving the hotel 2,870 rooms and more meeting, exhibit and public space.

In 1981, a decision was made to enter the field of cable television. Therefore, the company sold WSM-TV and created the Nashville Network, which went on the air on March 7, 1983. TNN set a cable television record for initial subscribers, with a base of nearly seven million homes. In less than five years, that grew to more than 50 million homes.

While Opryland USA was evolving, National Life was acquired by the American General Corporation. American General sold the Opryland USA companies on September 1, 1983 to Gaylord Broadcasting Company of Dallas, and a new company was born—Opryland USA Inc. Opryland USA Inc. and Gaylord Broadcasting Company are parts of the Oklahoma Publishing Company, which is owned by Edward L. Gaylord of Oklahoma City. In making the announcement, E. W. "Bud" Wendell, president and chief executive officer of Opryland USA Inc. remarked, "People who enjoy the Grand Ole Opry and Opryland's special kind of entertainment can rest assured that the Gaylord organization wants nothing more than to see those traditions of entertainment prosper and grow."

Acquisition by Edward Gaylord heightened the pace of growth. In December 1983, plans were announced for a $12 million paddlewheeler showboat that could carry 1,200 passengers on the Cumberland River, which flows beside the Opryland complex. The boat, the General Jack-

The curtain rises—followed by a fast fiddle tune, an enthusiastic crowd, intricate squaredancing—and the Grand Ole Opry eagerly begins another historic evening.

son, was christened by Mr. Gaylord's wife, Thelma, in ceremonies at Nashville's Riverfront Park on July 3, 1985. It immediately became one of Nashville's most popular attractions.

Another significant addition to Opryland USA came in 1985 with the purchase of Acuff-Rose, Nashville's first music publishing company. From Acuff-Rose has evolved the Opryland Music Group. Acuff-Rose was founded by Opry star Roy Acuff and songwriter/entertainer Fred Rose in 1942, and its catalog of copyrighted songs includes country and pop standards by songwriters such as Hank Williams, Pee Wee King, Dallas Frazier, Roy Orbison and the Everly Brothers.

Other components of Opryland USA Inc. have evolved through the years. Gaylord Syndicom, a component created in 1984, develops television shows for syndication, and is responsible for "Hee Haw," the long-running country music and entertainment show, one of the most successful shows in syndication history.

In 1988, the syndicated Music Country Radio Network was re-structured as TNNR. And in September 1990, TNN acquired the Country Music Television Network (CMT). That same year, E. W. Wendell, President and Chief Executive Officer of Gaylord Entertainment Company (NYSE:GET), announced the corporation would be broadcasting CMT in Europe and the United Kingdom. Other elements of the corporation include Opryland Productions Tape Duplicating Service; Grand Ole Opry Sightseeing Tours; and the beautiful 18 hole Springhouse Golf Course.

In 1994, the Ryman Auditorium reopened as a performing/television venue after a $8.5 million renovation. The famous theater offers a full schedule of evening entertainment, and serves as an historic museum during the day. That same year the Wildhorse Saloon opened on Nashville's historic Second Avenue. The Wildhorse features a horseshoe-shaped balcony overlooking a 3,000 square foot dance floor. Approximately 1,400 guests can enjoy great music, fun and country dancing. And to make sure the guests at Opryland can travel in style to downtown Nashville, Opryland's 100-passenger River Taxis provide a most unique way to navigate the winding Cumberland River.

The Grand Old Opry is, and has always been, entertainment, pageantry, vaudeville, and the music of all the people packaged into one presentation. The rapport between the Opry artist and the audience is unlike anything else in the world, whether the listener be at the Opry House, tuned to WSM's Clear Channel Frequency (650) that spans the United States, or watching each Saturday night on TNN.

The music is genuine, down-to-earth, and honest. It is realism. And, as Judge Hay explained once, "The principal appeal of the Opry is a homey one. It sends forth the aroma of bacon and eggs frying on the kitchen stove on a bright spring morning. That aroma is welcomed all the way from Maine to California."

—Jerry Strobel